John Gale was born in E[...] [...] [...] [...] [...] of four brothers. He was [...] [...] [...] [...] at seventeen joined the Coldstream Gu[...] [...] [...]nding the latter part of the war in Germany. He served in Palestine from 1945 to 1947 and spent a year seconded to the Transjordan Frontier Force. After demobilization he lived for a time in Paris, then returned to England, where he began a successful career in journalism.

In 1950 he married Jill Robertson; they had three children. Shortly after his marriage he started to write for the *Observer*, where he remained as regular reporter and foreign correspondent for twenty years, writing on events in Egypt, North Africa, the Far East and Europe, and on domestic affairs. He later spent some time in Hong Kong working for the *Asia Magazine*. His novel *The Family Man* appeared in 1968; he also wrote two travel books, *Travels with a Son* (1972), and *Camera Man*, an account of his experience in Hong Kong, published posthumously in 1979. John Gale died in London, in 1974.

CLEAN YOUNG ENGLISHMAN

John Gale

New Introduction by
Alan Ross

THE HOGARTH PRESS
LONDON

To Jill

Published in 1988 by
The Hogarth Press
30 Bedford Square, London WC1B 3RP

First published in Great Britain by Hodder and Stoughton 1965
Copyright © John Gale 1965
Introduction copyright © Alan Ross 1987

All rights reserved. No part of this publication may be re-
produced, stored in a retrieval system, or transmitted in any
form, or by any means, electronic, mechanical, photocopying,
recording or otherwise, without the prior permission of the
publisher.

A CIP catalogue record for this book
is available from the British Library

ISBN 0 7012 0776 0

Printed in Finland by
Werner Söderström Oy

INTRODUCTION

Clean Young Englishman was first published by Hodder and Stoughton in the autumn of 1965, and by Coward-McCann in the United States the following summer. At the time of its publication John Gale had been on the staff of the *Observer* for a dozen years, his twenty-year career on that paper coinciding with its golden period.

Clean Young Englishman was described by its original publishers as a book that 'seems to epitomise a whole generation'. Such a comment could fairly be made about Richard Hillary's *The Last Enemy*, perhaps, but though John Gale's book has much in common with Hillary's tone, background and manner, his attitude is altogether more idiosyncratic. Where Hillary's disillusion with war was romantic in nature, Gale's crack-up was rather that of a sceptic, disconcerted to find his happy-go-lucky, conventional and comfortable upbringing ultimately inadequate. His reactions to events, and his attitude towards himself, were by no means those common to his generation. Through a genetic fault, as much as anything else, he was unable to go along with tribal beliefs and behaviour. Nature, rather than conviction, made him non-conformist.

Although the prologue to *Clean Young Englishman* gives an unnervingly brilliant description of the physical sensations of mania and depression – 'when I am manic my beard and fingernails grow faster. In depression, my hair lies down; when I am manic it stands up electrically, catching sensations like antennae' – the first half of the book itself offers no suggestions of the untoward. Yet because in the prologue the reader has been alerted to future shock treatment and drug therapy, and been confided in about the author's superstitious and obsessive nature, his compulsively ritualistic daily habits, a shadow is cast over experiences that might otherwise have seemed, if not idyllic, at least more agreeable than most people's of his age. What gives *Clean Young Englishman* its particular quality is that, as the story progresses and the shadows begin to obliterate the earlier sunny atmosphere, the writing loses none of its vigour and fizz. It is not easy to be funny about mental breakdown, but because John Gale was an acute observer of the bizarre and surreal, he manages to make horrible experiences seem almost as comic as when, staying with a school friend, the family handyman conscientiously ironed his trousers in which a banana had been accidentally left.

During his army service an adjutant, noticing that Gale swung his arms excessively when walking, remarked 'Johnny, people that swing their arms like that go mad young.'

It is that sort of observation which hangs upsettingly over the years that *Clean Young Englishman* otherwise so entertainingly covers. John Gale's accounts of Abinger Hill, his prep. school, Stowe, where he was briefly taught by John Davenport, and the Coldstream Guards, are fairly perfunctory, but even here there is not a dull page, not an observation that does not have quirky originality and insight. As an Officer Cadet Gale is invited to a dance at Windsor Castle and dances, ineptly and rather drunk, with the future Queen. After a long silence she asks, 'Are you at Sand'urst?' to which, their only exchange of conversation, Gale replies 'No, Ma'am, Mons Barracks.'

The war was pretty much over by the time John was commissioned, but after a few weeks in Germany he went to Palestine and then, in order to learn Arabic, joined the Transjordan Frontier Force 'a Beau Geste outfit that wore red cummerbunds and black kalpaks made of Persian lamb.'

It was in Galilee that his euphoric squadron-commander, a classicist and future diplomat, called him 'a clean young Englishman'. 'God help us,' he said to Gale on one occasion, 'I can see your happy home: welcomes, a spaniel, an old nanny, and a faithful retainer in a green baize coat. You make me sick, Thucydides knew better.'

At the age of twenty-one John Gale was demobilized, having declined to stay on in the Coldstream as a regular officer. The rest of his book, almost exactly half of it, shows how far from the truth was his squadron-commander's prophecy. Marriage, a stint on the *Sunday Express*, and his years on the *Observer* form the background, but we know the reality from the prologue. What happens to the potentially 'clean young Englishman' may be distressing to read about, but few accounts of the process of breakdown have been so illuminating in detail and so absolutely free of pretentiousness and jargon. It is precisely in its expression of how his own experiences differed from the general run of others of his generation that makes *Clean Young Englishman* so honest and remarkable a book.

The story that *Clean Young Englishman* tells – that of a talented journalist who suddenly went crazy – was continued in what purported to be a novel, but which was scarcely disguised autobiography, *The Family Man*, published in 1968. There was one other book to appear in Gale's lifetime, *Travels with a Son*, the account of a five-month journey through Africa. At his death in 1974 he left behind the manuscript of a second novel, *Camera Man*, eventually revised and pruned by an *Observer* colleague, John Heilpern, and published in 1979.

Such a summary does not take into account the work that Gale did for the *Observer*, which was highly individual and of an extraordinary variety. He was essentially a journalist, hardly a novelist at all; his allegiance was to the truth, as he saw and only too intensely felt it, not to the creation of plot or character. About madness, he was, and wrote like, an expert.

For all the descriptive brilliance and passionate commitment of his reporting, when concerned with issues that engaged him, John Gale was also something of a narcissist. A defender of suede shoes (the subject of his first article for the *Observer*), he gave his appearance, clothes and moods the same close attention that he gave to the subjects of his interviews.

His books were all written after his first bad breakdown, on his return from Algeria in 1957, and, apart from the travel book, were haunted by the precariousness of his condition and its effect on himself, his wife and his children. Marriage and family were at the centre of his writing and described his own, whether perched in Hampstead, Provence – the scene of *The*

Family Man – or Hong Kong, where much of *Camera Man* takes place, with an honesty that was at times painful.

There is much pain in his books, as there was indeed in him as a person, but what might in less gifted hands have made for melancholy or monotonous writing was redeemed by his lightness of touch and his sense of the farcical. He often felt himself a cold man, out of tune with life, but usually the affectionate, responsive side of his nature came to the rescue. He really looked at people and at his surroundings, and as a result the characters and places in his books are convincing and memorable.

All you need to know about John Gale is in his books. While it is sometimes a mistake to identify a writer too closely with his fictional narrator, in Gale's case there is no dissemblance. He looked like what he was, except, on the occasions when it surfaced, for the fatal flaw. Whether you saw him at the *Observer* offices or in a pub, at a cricket match or at a party, there was no mistaking the sort of background and person. After demobilization Gale had gone to Paris and attended lectures at the Sorbonne, in the process learning to speak fluent French. ·

All this was readily accessible from him in conversation, for he was, superficially anyway, as open as he looked. He was floppy-haired and fair, handsome in a big boned, easy, smiling fashion, slightly teasing in manner, with a faint undercurrent of competitiveness. When I first met him he looked, with his bright-eyed, joking, obtrusively physical presence, about as far removed from a candidate for breakdown as you could possibly imagine. He had, moreover, one of those free and easy personalities that ensured popularity at all levels. He may himself have needed and craved affection, but he was not niggardly with it either.

My own time working for the *Observer*, 1950-72, began a year or two before John's and ended slightly later. But for most of the fifties and sixties we were colleagues, sometimes meeting weekly, sometimes not for several months or even years. I never myself saw him low in spirits, though there was occasionally a certain unease about him, a tension, which I put down to restlessness. He was the sort of person who needed a lot of exercising, like certain breeds of dog.

In those early days I wrote a number of Notebooks for the paper, from Germany and Italy, before becoming its cricket correspondent. John, whose main reporting was to be foreign, often wrote on the sports pages when he was in London, 'profiles' of jockeys, cricketers, skiers, tennis players, racing drivers and boxers. As a consequence, our journalistic ways often crossed. We met, too, at cricket matches, the *Observer* running a fairly ramshackle Sunday team for which we both occasionally played. John remarks more than once in his books that he hated to lose and was an ungracious loser, but that side of him, if it was true, had no chance to shine in such desultory affairs.

Then, out of the blue one winter, I received a call from the Foreign Editor: could I go out at once to North Africa for a few weeks? John Gale, who had been covering the Algerian war, was ill and had to come home. What was more, he was in no state to talk to me. Instead, I had to make do with re-reading John's despatches, which were of a fraught and violent nature.

From the misery of that time, his acute distress at the butchery and torture, John never properly recovered, though in between breakdowns he spent ten years writing for the paper, as a rule, except for an unfortunate assignment to Formosa, on less exacting domestic events.

Although John had made his name as a sympathetic interviewer of dropouts and down-and-outs, of misfits and eccentrics, he was then allotted the task of writing up visiting celebrities. Looking though his scrapbook of those days recently I noticed that, in the space of a year, he wrote longish pieces on such disparate characters as Lord Nuffield and Groucho Marx, Sandie Shaw and Louis Armstrong, John Huston and Humphrey Lyttelton, Tommy Steele and Donald Campbell, Kurt Hahn and Charlie Chaplin, Marlene Dietrich and Wedgwood Benn, Jeanne Moreau and the Chief Scout, all this at the same time as covering elections and dog-shows. Skilful at drawing even the least co-operative people out and letting them do the talking, John's innate voyeurism and genuine curiosity enabled him to create fascinating portraits by the most economical and unobtrusive methods. After the Groucho Marx profile had appeared its subject wrote to David Astor, the paper's editor. 'The reason I was so co-operative with John Gale is a very simple one. He happens to be a very nice fellow, but I must say slightly unreliable. He promised to send me two Sunday pieces from the *Observer*, neither of which have arrived. I don't know whether to attribute this to the Geneva Conference, the Wimbledon results, or just sheer lassitude.'

Scott Fitzgerald, that most articulate commentator on breakdown, observed after his own crack-up that one was rather like a cracked plate, which has to be 'kept in service as a household necessity' but which 'can never again be warmed on the stove nor shuffled with the other plates in the dish pan; it will not be brought out for company, but it will do to hold crackers late at night or to go into the ice-box under left-overs.' It was a feeling not unknown to John or, for that matter, to myself.

John had his worst breakdown, as described at the end of *Clean Young Englishman*, after accepting an invitation from the State Department, which had been impressed by his writings on Algeria. Everything about America, in his odd, wild, occasionally heavy-drinking state, appalled him. He became quite unhinged, and soon after his return was obliged to spend four months in a clinic, sedated, drugged and finally given electric shock treatment.

My last meeting with John was in Hong Kong in 1972. He had gone out there for a year, taking his wife Jill and their three children, to work for the *Asia Magazine*. He had that 'cracked plate' fragility Scott Fitzgerald spoke of and with whose signs I was familiar. He did not, though seem unhappy, plain though it was that his high-flying days as a foreign correspondent were over and that, like a rare species, he needed protection.

We made a trip to Macao together and he was, as he could be, wonderful company, all the better for being relaxed and calm, rather than enervated. He quotes Jill in *Clean Young Englishman* as saying to him: 'Why can't you be more natural and take things in a straight-forward way,' and now he was being just that.

It did not, unfortunately, last. They came home and Johnny began work on *Camera Man*, a novel in which, using his Hong Kong life and a love affair as background, he discusses the pulls between affection and infidelity, allegiance and treachery, security and the need to escape. There was something essentially innocent and rather trusting about his own character, but in his writing he worried over what seemed to him damaging flaws of temperament and behaviour.

The novel went reasonably well but the depressions returned. He began to experience the unpleasant sensations that usually heralded disaster. Drugs could control them but he found the dependence on them increasingly distasteful. He made a vague attempt at suicide and then, on Hampstead Heath a week later, a successful one. He was forty-eight.

When *Clean Young Englishman* was published it was perceptively reviewed in the *Observer* by John Wain (with, as it happens, Gavin Maxwell's autobiographical *The House of Elrig*). Wain drew attention to Gale's dislike of rationalisation and discourse. 'His style is *pointilliste*, innumerable small dabs of colour coming together in a previously undiscovered harmony. As in Imagist poetry, image and cadence are carefully chosen, generalisation and deduction avoided.' William Trevor in the *Listener*, observed that John Gale was a man 'to whom things happen,' and much of whose skill lay in an ability to 'retail and link his precisely recalled detail, and in spiking everything with an occasional note of ferocity.'

Most of the reviews, however, admiring as they properly were of the quality of the writing, concerned themselves with the problem of what, precisely, pushed a person of such evident resources and advantages so terrifyingly over the edge. They came up with no suggestions. John's experiences were not unique, and the fact that many survived them without lasting damage can be put down to luck, heredity or personality. There, but for the grace of God, some may feel. 'I am what they call a manic-depressive,' John wrote after his second breakdown, 'they love to label us. When I am manic I am close on six feet tall; when I am depressed I am not much over five feet ten inches.' It is a typical Gale remark, no doubt founded on meticulous observation. His situation turned out to be an extreme one, which he described with heart-breaking candour.

Alan Ross, London 1987

Foreword

On my desk is a shape of foreboding. I made it in a clinic when I was crazy: they called it occupational therapy. The shape, which has a red-and-black finish, is like a seven-legged mechanical monster; it has mouth and eye (reminiscent of a spanner's) and, between the legs, six gaps which, together with the mouth and eye, represent the musical scale. It is in some way prehistoric.

When I made the shape I wrote this rather Biblical note:

Make the key of life. Make it the shape it has to be, the shape that echoes all the senses: visual, musical, sensual, and the way of all life. Make the surface rough, so that it can catch the stuff of life: seed blown by the wind, humus and earth; make it so that it can feel, breathe, and drink water; let it be rough on the surface and not smooth, so that it can catch and nourish life; for if smooth and siliceous it is a reversal of nature, it is the anti-life, the bringer of fire and burning, of Martian and Saturnalian shapes. Let it be ear, mouth and eye, the insect's nest, the Minotaur's labyrinth; the synthesis of that lost insect and animal paradise from where we all came.

The first shape I made, to fulfil these conditions, blew up in the kiln when it was being baked, and destroyed the pots of my fellow-patients, who were furious. A young nurse had helped me make the shape, since I was in bed and almost paralysed by drugs. We must have left air bubbles in the clay. The fate of that shape, and the conception of it, seemed typical of my life.

I made another shape, this time unaided, since the shape had to be made: this time the kiln broke down, and the shape came out a dull black, the frozen incarnation of my devil. I brought this shape home when I left the clinic. It so upset Jill, my wife, that I stuck plaster on parts of its surface, painted the plaster red, and varnished it. The red took some of the foreboding from the black shape; and Jill allowed it to stay on my desk, where it lies now, a talisman.

Prologue

One night this year, on the walk home from the Underground in the falling snow, I had to lean against the wall of the crematorium where my father went up in smoke. I had had a few drinks. The wind pierced my short, old-fashioned black coat that had belonged to my grandfather. When I walked on a little unsteadily in the dark on the creaking snow, a girl passed on the other side of the road, her high black boots gleaming faintly. She looked across at me, and then went on in the bitter cold.

Our three children had measles; Jill was tired. The wind moaned beneath the doors; we were keeping fires going day and night, and the insects cried in the blazing logs. Our house is small, virtually a cottage, among terraced houses built, originally, for artisans; the road is the appendix of the suburb, with wealthier houses not far off. I like our house: scarcely a piece of furniture, not a picture, carpet, or curtain did we choose ourselves; all was given or passed on by relatives; all, or almost all, is incongruous, tasteless, but well used.

At times I feel the small house is the centre of the world. It seems a turning-point for aircraft coming in to land at London Airport. Their engines change pitch as they come in from east and west, booming and whining through the dusk, their navigation lights winking hope. I like the Viscounts: they are clean, with little waste in their line. About the big swept-wing jets, Russian and American, there is something unsettling; no one that lives beneath those wings can feel at ease; there is a hint of the pterodactyl; it is a rapacious line, touching something far back in the memory. When I lie in bed I distrust all aircraft: where are they going? People should stay at home. I prefer the sound of trains far off at night, the clink of shunting in a cold siding.

The street lamps of our suburb are strange: flaring orange on

9

tall swan's-necked stalks of concrete. On the way home in the dark I look down on the orange patterns stretching into the wintry bloom, and sometimes I enjoy them; but not always, for this strange light must be doing something to our perception. When the lamps first went up one summer, a family down the road complained to a local councillor about them. The councillor was a Liberal, and the family told him they had helped elect him. He thought they were making a fuss about nothing. He said a few words, and then took the family to see his rose garden: he gave the mother a pink rose. It was getting dark. The mother said to the councillor: 'Now come and see what your lamps do to your roses.' She took the councillor under a lamp and held out the pink rose to him: under the orange glare it was a dirty white, veined with black.

'I never knew,' said the councillor. 'I never knew.'

What are cars doing to us? What about those endless pavements? Think of roads: standing on a road you are linked to all the other roads in the country and to the people on them.

I am what they like to call a manic-depressive; they love to label us. When I am manic I am close on six feet tall; when I am depressed I am not much over five feet ten inches. If I am manic, my watch gains five minutes a week; if I am depressed, it loses five minutes a week. When I am manic my beard and finger-nails grow faster. In depression, my hair lies down; when I am manic it stands up electrically, catching sensations like antennae. How do bald men do? Should not bald men be obtuse, unreceptive and alone? Yet it is true that bald men often make up for the lack of hair on their heads by being immensely hairy elsewhere – even having hair on their backs.

In no mood is my hair tall and fuzzy. A publican once pointed out to me a man with hair like this, sitting in his saloon bar and said 'People with that sort of hair can give you a lot of trouble.' They also tend to give off blue flashes when they undress in the dark on frosty nights.

I well understand what happened to Samson; for when I have my hair cut I feel weak and lifeless and without ideas. I visit the barber rarely. (When I was small, barbers quite often used to snip a large mole behind my left ear, which bled profusely. 'Oh, it's quite all right,' I'd say, to reassure them. Yet it was careless.)

Electricity is God; so I thought when my mind was unhinged. Madness is a time of perception, of reality. I saw evil then, and knew it. I saw men as descended from animals: there were pig men, rat men, snake men. But, above all, pig men, with evil grey faces: a few years ago one of them, an old reporter, old yet ageless, with a face that was almost a shiny green, sat his huge bottom, forcibly, between me and a girl journalist, separating us, as we sat talking together before the start of some infernal meeting at Maidstone. The girl and I were talking and we were happy. He sat down between us just as the meeting was starting, when it was impossible to do anything about him. He behaved as though he disliked our being together; he was anti-life. I never saw that girl again. The meeting was near Maidstone Prison. There were silent birds sitting in the trees and on the houses not far from the prison walls; no bird sang and no bird ever flew over the prison that day. The air near the prison was dead.

When madness goes, your perception dies: what perception one had then! They say the brain gives out electrical impulses: certainly extra-sensory perception has seemed a reality to me. I once met a man I had never met before when I was manic, and I was able to tell him his address, which I could not have known before: Rossetti Mansions, Flood Street, Chelsea. He was a painter, a fighter pilot in the war, and had a burnt face, a mask. I caught the thoughts of others in the air then. But people do not always forgive you for what you see in this state: for you see what is behind a man's eye.

When manic I feel fine, but I get into trouble. Depression is safer and lasts longer. Five years ago I was feeling like this:

Every morning I get up a little too late, and have to hurry, though I am not good at hurrying. Often I feel heavy in the legs, and stink of self-pity. I lean over the cot of my small daughter, Kiki, and have a few words with her. She passes up things for me to admire: a button; the torn remnant of an out-of-date book token; a feather pulled from her pillow and carefully guarded.

I go into the bathroom to shave, and notice in the flaking mirror those signs of the flesh sagging and shrinking round the eyes; I pull the skin at the outside corners of the eyes and then let it go, noticing that it regains its position slowly; I can make out the line of the eye socket beneath the blue skin. Stuffed into a small ventilator grille high in the bathroom's outside wall is a yellowed newspaper with, upside down, this headline: WHOSE FOOT IS ON THE BRAKE?

Well, whose is?

My mother-in-law stuffed that paper into the grille more than four years ago, on the bitter February night my son, James, was born. Was she trying to give me a message? I am thirty-two.

At the breakfast table there is a conversation that is a product of the monotonous and careful religious differentiation at the local primary school.

'Are you Chriss-tian?' Joanna, aged six, asks Kiki, who is two. Without waiting for an answer, she adds: 'You're Jewish. I know you are.'

'No,' says Kiki. 'I'm a flower.'

'I'll never cut you down,' says James.

Kiki to Joanna: 'I'll give you a butterfly when you get married.'

I was going round in circles. Three years later, after drugs and electric shock (which impairs your memory for some months), I felt like this:

When you get to thirty-five, you ought to know where you're going; I'm no more certain now than when I was twenty. Perhaps it is the winter that brings on these thoughts. Rain and black damp have returned, making us all curl up and turn inwards; at this time of year I realize what the English are, and why. It is raw weather, and I marvel that people can survive it. I look out on our small garden, a waste of mud and leaves. How can a man work outside, against the elements, at such a time of year?

In the mornings I stay in bed until the very last moment, hiding. Then I get up with a fair rush, only fair, because I have no energy in the mornings. When shaving in the cold mirror I look at the blue hollows round my eyes, and I think: 'This is the face of a man on the run.' The walls of the bathroom are peeling, the window-frames are green with mould: the woodwork will rot soon, that's certain, and most of the house is the same. Perhaps you know the feeling. Still stuffed into the small ventilator grille high in the outside wall of the bathroom is that yellowed newspaper, with, upside down, the head-line: WHOSE FOOT IS ON THE BRAKE? I've given up wondering whose foot is.

My first duty in the morning is to take James to school. I gulp a cup of tea first, if I have time. James wears a thick tweed coat, far too big for him, and secures it with a highly unsatisfactory leather belt. The blue school cap swamps him, but he likes it; his two-coloured fringe appears beneath the peak. The parents of this school like to keep up appearances, but we don't impress them. While I'm gulping that cup of tea, I tell James to run ahead, saying I shall catch him up. I know running is supposed to be bad for you first thing in the morning, particularly after a cup of tea. But what can you do? James can run pretty fast, and I seldom catch him till he's turned the corner by the allotments. Labourers employed by the council are clearing the wasteland on either side of the stream here: first they cleared the lank bushes and the bottles, tins and old bicycle frames; then they ploughed the ground. Now they are burning what they can: some of it is fine wood, and the embers give off blue smoke and a good smell. James likes to stop and watch; that is how I catch him up. Sometimes he takes my hand here; he will never do so if he thinks his friends are about. Walking to the main road we pass a lot of people scurrying to the bus stop, the insects' rush to work.

The main road is hard to cross, for at this hour of the morning it is alive with traffic: the cars of desperate businessmen, heading for London. We keep well back from the puddles on the side of the road, for fear we shall get splashed; then, when there is a gap in the traffic, we run across. Sometimes I feel irresponsible, for we cut it pretty fine, just in front of cars.

Walking up towards the school I keep a sharp lookout for dogs' messes: it is that kind of pavement; riddled with them. I wish people would control their dogs. At the same hour every morning we pass the same people coming down fast the other way, to catch a bus. I imagine one of them to have been an actress; she has wide-apart eyes, a pleasant loose face, dark hair, purple coat and black boots with high heels; about her there is an air of things past; perhaps she is now working in an office typing mindless documents.

The houses here are all small, semi-detached. One lawn has a family of gnomes in red-and-blue coats; James approves of them. Outside this house is a small, pale-blue car, not new: it is owned by a young couple I judge to be ambitious. He has a pointed face with flushed cheeks and slicked-down mousy hair. His shoes are brown and highly-polished, the last a sign of anxiety and ambition. These shoes are pointed and they glitter offensively as he walks along with a flat-footed mincing walk, toes turned outwards. He wears a tightly-belted fawn raincoat and carries a small briefcase. His wife is a big heavy-faced girl, sullen, unbeautiful, with a bun: I think she is the boss. She used to go with him to catch the bus, but now they have a baby, which is always swaddled in thick blue knitted garments. She holds up the baby to see him off at the front door every morning. I am sure this couple are voracious readers, always returning their books on time to the public library. What do they eat? Strong-tasting over-cooked mutton, I'd say, and a lot of mince on fried toast, enlivened with ketchup.

At the top of the road there is a pillar box, and the postman is always leaning against it by the time we arrive, waiting to collect the nine o'clock post. Children converge here from all directions, some of them accompanied by au pair girls, chattering, the German voices highest. Some children come in their fathers' serpentine cars; for ours is a suburb where people are keen to get on. One or two of the children are Indian, and they are brought to school by their grandmothers, peaceful ladies with overcoats over their saris. I take James to the school gates, and he runs in. He dislikes school.

I walk home to finish my breakfast. By this time Jill has taken our two small girls to their school in our van. This van is a problem; I am certain it will die on us soon, and we shall not have enough money to have it repaired; it will disintegrate slowly in the road outside our door.

Walking back, I try to savour the moment: a damp, raw morning, with a purple, misty bloom in the air; suburban chimneys and television aerials; a dripping oak wood ahead, with a recently-asphalted black path cutting through it, alien and incongruous; a church steeple; blackbirds chinking mournfully. On the far side of the main road are some odd, pollarded willows; they have an abrupt, lopped, V-shape, and one evening I saw them silhouetted against an orange sky, with a jet trail framed in the V of the centre tree.

I pass a little man with a pork-pie hat and rimless glasses. He says, 'Good morning. Not so good again.' He also wears a tightly-belted raincoat, not fawn, but grey. He owns a gents' outfitters. He is a good man, and has a good wife. She has pink cheeks and a round face, and was for many years a nanny with a large family. At last, when the children of the family had grown up, she left the family and married the little outfitter. When she was over forty, they had a child. It was a mongol. They adore it. Every Christmas she brings presents to our children.

Now forty is just ahead of me. Forty: it is unbelievable. I look into the mirror, noting my receding hair. Yoga seemed to be the answer once, and I learnt to stand on my head, spending five minutes like this each morning, feet and legs visible through the bedroom window: all part of the business of pulling oneself together. Some yogic instruction books say you must be careful about this exercise, since faulty technique can drive you crazy. Was this what happened to me? When I came out of the clinic after that breakdown – it was really a break-up – I gave up yoga, believing instead that the answer to life was to stretch the spine by hanging by one's arms. I started hanging for a minute each day from a branch of the rowan tree by our garden gate. Afterwards I would pick up James, then aged five or six, and make him hang there for a bit, too, so that my own performance looked entirely normal to passers-by. He would hang there with his Balaclava helmet over one eye, saying nothing. But soon the rowan (it is a lucky tree) died, perhaps killed by our ritual. Now I hold in my stomach. A friend of mine said, during a lunch-hour walk by the Thames: 'Do you ever concentrate on holding in your stomach? There may come a day when you'll regret it if you don't.'

Every day after breakfast I still walk to the Underground station, through the endless suburb, a sensible waste of privet hedges and well-polished Zodiacs, dying slowly to the cries of rag-and-bone men. In the central square, beyond the wide lawn lined with grotesquely-pollarded trees, is a church, a tall, cindery building whose sharp black spire looks charred and desolate. When there is the slightest wind, something tinkles high up on the roof of the church, though I have never discovered what it is.

Beyond the church is the crematorium, a landmark that I pass night and morning. Whenever I consider my life I think of the crematorium: when I was in Formosa, Egypt, or Algeria, the crematorium came up in my mind: an Oriental red-brick palace with a central tower that has a green copper cupola and two windows like large eyes: there are happy mourners; cynical undertakers who stub out their fags and compose their faces before driving in through the gates in upright hearses, the wreaths scattering a few petals on the damp pavement or the snow; the definitive trace of man.

'That's where people die,' said James one wet day several years ago.

'Oh?'

'Yes. Just die.'

A funeral cortège passed us then in ancient upright Rolls-Royces, the roof of the hearse piled with raw white lilies, glistening with raindrops.

'Those flowers are for the Queen,' said James.

Once this year, on the hard snow, a black cat coiled and uncoiled with electric tension against the crematorium's wrought-iron gates. A little farther on in the snow were drops of blood. Whose blood could this have been? At Golders Green Underground station that morning I was more than usually careful about what coins to use for my fare to Blackfriars. Sometimes I like certain coins, particularly old ones, believing them lucky, and keep them as long as possible: one is an Edwardian penny that went through an elephant; it is dated 1908, and King Edward's face on the coin is strangely dark, perhaps with anger at the experience, which lasted twenty-four hours; I was given the penny five years ago by the head keeper of elephants at the London Zoo.

I have always been superstitious. Sometimes, before I throw a piece of paper into the waste-paper basket, I say to myself: 'If this piece of paper doesn't land in the waste-paper basket first go, I shall have a wasted life.' Often the paper doesn't go in, and I try to ignore it; but for a few minutes I may have a slightly uneasy feeling. If I don't try too hard, and flip the piece of paper casually, it is more likely to land where I want it to. And if I am in a manic or elated mood, it seems to me that I can alter the trajectory of the paper in mid-air: when I have aimed too low, I have willed the paper to rise up, over the edge of the basket, for a good landing.

Another piece of superstition: I always used to keep in my breastpocket a grey handkerchief with a hole in it. I believed it lucky ever since I flew it from the top of the Eiffel Tower. Sometimes I think my clothes may be the most important thing about me, since I am almost entirely responsible for them (I am only about half responsible for my face). My clothes are not good, not careful, not well-kept; but they are there, day and night, on me, or on my chair in the bedroom, under the orange glow of the street lights, as I sleep. Their influence is strong.

Shoes are no problem. But they are important. A friend of mine once read *La Chartreuse de Parme* by Stendhal: it inspired him; he determined to change the direction of his life; in the end he just went out and bought himself a new pair of shoes.

Trousers can play a big part in life. They are seldom responsible for decisions that transform careers; but they can have a pervasive influence. However much some people scoff at the idea, it is undoubtedly true that baggy trousers deaden the imagination. Fine creases, too, are a worry, since at heart one is reluctant to spoil them by sitting down – particularly in damp weather.

My first long trousers coincided with my first train journey alone. It was 1936. I was put in the care of the guard and given a bunch of bananas to eat on the way. I was going to stay with a friend from school. His family had a handyman, a refugee from Germany, who was actually a lawyer. He was doing the job temporarily, and was very conscientious. He whisked away my trousers on the first night to press them; and he was so thorough that he ironed into them one of my bananas, left unthinkingly in a pocket in my anxiety to get out at the right station. When a banana is ironed into tweed it makes a dark, oily stain, which goes on spreading for a day or two.

At one time, in search of balance and the good life, not only did I wear the same clothes almost every day, but I also ate the same meal every day, usually in a Polish restaurant in Fleet Street: it was chicken (I think tinned) and apple pie with cream substitute. I thought an unchanging diet might lead to something.

In those days I never shaved on Sundays. But in the week I shaved with an electric razor, which, after a time, seemed to be changing my personality: something to do with sound waves, I imagined. Every morning, when I cleaned the razor, I emptied the peppery dust of my beard on to the bill of a hotel I had stayed at once in Brussels. Then I shook the bill out of the window, and watched the remnants of my beard float down on to the flower-bed below.

I spent a good deal of time at that period wondering what it would be like if all the food and drink I had ever eaten and drunk were to go slowly past on lorries. It became a preoccupation. How much bread would there be, how much beef and chocolate cake, how many cloves of garlic and pints of bitter? Above all, how much tinned chicken and apple pie? It was an interesting subject. I decided eventually that a lifetime's eating might look less impressive than you would think. But it would give you some idea of what you were made of.

Incidentally, that beard-dust I used to empty on to the flower bed must have taken root and grown into a plant. Some people said this could not happen, and that it was just old man's beard, or something like that; even I couldn't quite believe it. But a very strange plant did grow under the bedroom window: reddish, and a bit spiky. Jill, who knows about plants, couldn't place it. When you think of the way life must have started, well, anything is possible.

I gave up using an electric razor, and went back to soap and blade. But I was still going round in circles, spiralling; the coiled snake.

I have always cared what people thought and said of me. I have a broad face and grey-green eyes slanting down towards the outside; a long nose that still looks to me straight when I regard it in profile in two mirrors (though it was broken during the war by a Commando, a former London policeman, who swung at me with the back of his hand when I wasn't looking); and a chin that could, I think, be described as firm, though such things are deceptive. My teeth are good, and were nearly used once in a television advertisement. My long hair is receding a bit, and must be greying, though its colour hides this. I used to think of myself as fair, and was indeed almost white-haired when small, though my eyebrows were always strong and dark, so that they teased me, saying I used peroxide. My hair is still fairish, and fine, even floppy, but towards my ears it is unaccountably dark, almost black, and wiry: here, if you look carefully, so Jill tells me, you may find traces of grey and, particularly, red. On the few occasions I have grown a beard for a short time, it is a red-black beard, strong, and death to all razors. At certain times, Jill says, my hair is almost green.

My face is on the whole healthy-looking, quite often brown. I am just under six feet tall, broadish, not fat, even on the slim side, though big bones may hide this. I weigh about twelve stone. My hands, on small wrists, are large, flexible, and, except at games, impractical. I gesture with them often; the fingers are long, double-jointed, and a little knobbly from catching cricket balls. My feet are smallish and broad. I am active, and probably look it; but on occasions my forehead is wrinkled like that of an old elephant or exhausted lion: this is a characteristic of my mother's family, the Mackinnons. When I am manic and confident, my hair, as already stated, stands up, my mouth might be taken for strong, and is framed on each side by a deep cleft descending from the nostrils.

Almost every day I walk at least four miles, which helps me think. When walking fast, I tend to swing my arms excessively: twenty years ago an adjutant in the Army noticed this and said: 'Johnny, people that swing their arms like that go mad young.'

Part One

I was born near Edenbridge, in Kent, in flat country reeking of sheep and mangel-wurzels and echoing to the sad cry of peewits. It seems to me that the ghosts of the 1914-18 War lay heavy over it, and that the war was in my bones, though I was born seven years after it ended. We were nowhere near the coast, but France did not seem far, and the plaintive tune of 'Roses of Picardy' seemed to rustle in the poplars that lined the ponds and small brown river, smelling of mud and fish, near our beamed Elizabethan house. When I was small Poppy Day had a heavy significance.

People talked of the war often. My mother's first cousin was killed flying with the RFC: apparently he always flew low, taking great care not to harm civilians. When they sent back his uniform and personal things, his mother, my great-aunt, said: 'Oh, I smell the smell of him in his clothes.' My uncle was in that war, my father was too young.

I knew a man who always smoked cigarettes when he was gutting rabbits, because he had been gassed in the war, which somehow made the guts of the rabbits smell worse in his nostrils, and he smoked to drown the smell. He was a farm labourer, and had an antique motor-bike and sidecar, with carbide lamps that had a distinctive, prickly, gaseous odour, not unpleasant.

My first remembered sensation is of sucked leather, a bitter, depressing taste, that came from the straps of my pram. I can still smell the oilcloth interior of that pram: I did not like it.

Before I was two my mother was very ill, and had a serious operation performed by the only surgeon in England then capable of it: she was away many months, before making a complete recovery. At about this time my father gave her an Easter egg containing a black spaniel puppy called Susan, who grew large,

23

smelly, and enthusiastic, wagging her bottom and licking us all. I have had a horror of effusive dogs ever since.

At the back of our house were paths of stone flags lined with nasturtiums. I dropped a brick on a large toad on the central path almost as soon as I could walk. Across the farm track that divided our land were the orchard and kitchen garden with a wall on which grew peaches and nectarines. The farmer that lived at the end of the farm track dipped his sheep in a deep pit full of a yellow liquid that had a marvellous, tarry, disinfectant smell: but the sheep, poked under the surface with a stick like a hairless broom, struggled and thought they would drown.

Our gardener, Mr May, was old even then, though active. He had a thin, mischievous face and a garden shed that smelled of tarred string and sweet midge repellent. He was a gardener at heart, and I loved to watch his hands, with their long, ridged nails, as they planted, dibbled, tied up plants, and picked fruit. At his lunch-hour he would take my elder brother, Peter, and me into his cottage and read us 'Pip, Squeak and Wilfred' from the newspaper as we sat on his knee, while he sipped tea and ate bread and cheese. Popski, in 'Pip, Squeak and Wilfred', who had a cloak and beard and placed smoking bombs, was my first idea of a communist, though he may actually have been an anarchist.

My father used to go beagling, and would return, soaked, for a mustard bath, which we sometimes shared with him. Then he would have a plate of bread-and-milk with brown sugar. He gave up beagling suddenly after seeing the large and terrified eyes of a hare that, running in a circle, passed close by him.

When still very small, Peter somehow got mole traps, selling the mole skins for 2d. each; but two farmer's boys rolled in the traps with a horse and heavy roller and, when we protested, said 'bugger', the first time I heard the word.

One Christmas a vague godfather gave Peter and me a front and a back lamp for our tricycles: Peter took the front lamp and I used the back lamp on the front of my tricycle, though the small red glow was inadequate: one night I tricycled into our pond and was pulled out, covered with mud, weed and rotting leaves, by my parents, who came down the drive at that moment in a bull-nosed Morris.

Peter was good with animals, I wasn't. He knew almost every bird and beast. Walking along a path in a wood, he would suddenly stop, holding up his finger, sniff, and then hiss: 'Fox! Smell it.' There would be that sinister, tangy scent of a dox-fox, giving us gooseflesh, and filling us with fear and delight.

A lively woman of German descent who wore bowler hats used to visit us and take us for rides in her reverberating Bentleys, which she raced at Brooklands. She also had racehorses, and in a stable at Lingfield one of them took in its teeth a mouthful of my hair, which it mistook for straw, and lifted me off the ground, so that I swung in the air.

The house of our neighbours was separated from ours only by an old wall. Near the wall at the bottom of our garden were dark yew trees in which a tawny owl sat and occasionally hooted. The neighbours had a model farm. One day their chick-incubators caught fire in the cellar of their house, and Peter and I climbed the wall and went into the house, amid confusion, to have a look: Peter bent over and kissed a fireman's shining helmet as the fireman knelt down to aim his hose into the steaming cellar. A tall woman with short grey hair, brown beret, and corduroy coat and trousers ran the neighbours' chicken farm, and the fire upset her.

Usually Peter and I slept in a long nursery with a dark-beamed ceiling. The fireplace had a fireguard with thick black diagonal wires and a polished brass rail. We woke in the mornings to the sound of Mr May clunking buckets in the yards and calling the ducks.

In the afternoons I was put to rest in the spare bedroom; I was bored. I plucked feathers from the pale blue eiderdown of my bed and stuffed them into a knot-hole in a thick old beam in the wall.

One year the Territorials held anti-aircraft manœuvres in the Green Field across the road at the end of our drive: they were friendly men, and their uniforms seemed thick, brown and prickly; they manned searchlights and crude-looking devices, like metal-and-rubber ears, with which they tried to pick up the approach of ancient puttering aircraft. Our parents said they would wake us at midnight and take us out to see the search-lights in action; but, because we were sleeping soundly, they never did.

Almost always, over the sad, grey land, there was the cry of peewits. One winter the hedges disappeared beneath the snow, and the waterfall on the river by the mill froze like the melted wax of massive candles. More often only the brown puddles in our yellow mud-and-gravel drive froze hard: they had white air bubbles below the surface of the ice. Peter and I were walking with smoking breath in the drive before breakfast one sunny frosty morning, cracking the ice into splinters with our heels. Our parents were away, staying up at Crockham Hill with our grand-parents, my mother's father and mother. Suddenly my grand-father's great upright Vauxhall, driven by his chauffeur, appeared in the drive: it had a speaking-tube, lined grey whip-cord seats and a glass partition between passengers and driver. The chauffeur drove us up to the large stone house at Crockham Hill, where we each ate a goose-egg for breakfast.

The house at Crockham Hill had a marvellous view over the Weald of Kent: a train would occasionally puff across the green valley, neat white smoke unfolding from it, and that rhythmic sound of regularity, continuation, and far-off places would come up to us, as we drank coffee and my grandfather smoked a cigar: Ashdown Forest and the South Downs would be blue in the distance. My grandfather, who was for some years Chairman of Lloyd's, had had the house built before the first war from the yellow stone quarried on the spot. The house smelled wonder-fully clean, had many bathrooms, and polished wood floors with Persian rugs. There was a covered bridge across the drive to my grandmother's large workroom, which had a scent of drying herbs: she was a great gardener, and spent much time stirring strange brews for her soil; when we went to a certain part of the country, she would instruct us to bring back a particular wild flower for one of her potions. She hated chemical fertilizers, and campaigned against their use. She had a large telescope on a tripod with which she studied the moon.

The garden at Crockham Hill was large, with a swimming pool. Below was the farm, one of my grandfather's hobbies, with

26

cattle, pigs, oasthouses and barns full of floury sacks of wonder-ful-smelling feed, oats and barley. We used to go mousing in the barns, searching for mice behind the sacks, an exciting sport, but terrible if we actually laid out a mouse with a stick. The foreman of the farm was called Hammy: he was a wise man with a round face like an apple, a cap on the back of his head, thick belt, and clinking hobnail boots.

One of the best things about the farm was its cream. In the early days milkmaids carried the milk in pails yoked to their shoulders up to the dairy opposite the back door of my grand-parents' house, where they skimmed it and churned the butter, producing a cool, rich, yellow smell.

At Christmas we had lunch at home. But we went to Crock-ham Hill for tea and afterwards the opening of presents from the Christmas tree. 'It's just what I wanted,' we gasped as we tore at our parcels. We used to spend Christmas night at our grand-parents' house. Traditionally on Boxing Day there was ferret-ing in the warrens of the farm with the farm hands, organized by my uncle Mick, my mother's younger brother. They shot and netted the rabbits. I didn't care for it; but the lunch of cold turkey, as we stood among the elder bushes by the rabbit warrens in the cold mist, was good.

Rabbits suffered in summer, too, at the cutting of the corn: as the fine-smelling dust of the harvest rose into the air in the even-ing sun, and the clattering reaper cut the last rectangle of stand-ing corn in the centre of the field, you could see the silhouettes of the rabbits crouching there, quivering, their ears flat, in the uncut stalks, as the reaper came nearer and nearer: at the very last they bolted, to be shot; or chased to death by boys with sticks.

Mick was well-covered, with a wide face, brown hair, wrinkled brow, and a lazy voice. As a young man he had a succession of aircraft, and would fly to France and bring back loaves of bread. In pageants at Edenbridge he took leading parts, and would play the roles of both the chief of the Excise men and the leader of the smugglers, wearing a red handkerchief round his head and leap-ing on and off galloping horses.

The vicar of Edenbridge was a relative of ours by marriage,

and one of his daughters had lessons with us: to me vicarages mean red brick, mutton, and damp, dark laurel bushes above black earth paths.

Two great-aunts lived not far off in a square Victorian house near Lingfield. They used to fetch us for the day in their Baby Austin with a black canvas hood. We sometimes met their nephew, a wiry, dark boy who was as skilful as a gipsy at poaching pike and pheasant. Charcoal-burners, medieval beings, lived in a smoking hut made of hazel poles and shaped like a wigwam in the woods near the great-aunts. Are there charcoal-burners left in England now? At the back of the great-aunts' house we once found a horse-mushroom bigger than a soup plate. They had a moss-covered tennis court under the trees and a weedy pond, its surface tickled by water-boatmen: on Armistice Day one year I stood rigidly by the pond for the two minutes' silence announced by a distant factory hooter.

Peter and I used also to visit an old man who wore a white hat, made us clay pipes, and taught us to smoke. One day we smoked a large box of Fribourg and Treyer's cigarettes belonging to my father. The box was black with gold lettering. After we had smoked the whole box, puffing desperately, we smoked *The Times*, and were sick. The governess put us to bed. I have scarcely smoked since. Our governess was a good woman, with cropped dark hair, who wore long dresses. She played 'Men of Harlech' on the piano. She used to take us to search for flint arrowheads, and had a certain way of riding her bicycle, squeaking along in front, very upright, while I pedalled my tricycle desperately to keep up. But she allowed me to ride for miles by myself on the road to a large oak. There was little traffic, except for huge, polished, chain-driven steam wagons, with solid tyres, the heat from their funnels wrinkling the air like the heat in mid-summer above a field of wheat. Near the oak was a Regency house with a pond full of water snakes. Some years later, during the Battle of Britain, a Spitfire went straight into the ground at five hundred miles an hour by the great oak, leaving on the earth round the hole a burnt ring like the ashes of a wood fire.

Often the river flooded the flat land. After he came back from the City in the evenings my father would take us down in our

dressing gowns in the dicky of his car to see the floods. A car
stalled in a flood was a good sight. At week-ends we spent a lot
of time chasing fire engines dashing to haystack fires. There were
countless haystack fires, and we flew after the gleaming jangling
fire engines. Sitting in the house, my father would cock his head,
hold up his right hand with the forefinger pointing, and exclaim,
'Listen! fire engine.' We would run to the car, and drive after
the fire engine's bell. I shall never forget the charred, bitter-sweet,
sinister smell of a burning haystack.

My father could be terrifying when we were young; yet he
was fun. Almost my earliest memory of him is his throwing and
kicking a ball high into the air for us by a tall clump of pines in
Ashdown Forest. Once, just before we set out on a Sunday walk,
he had to destroy one of our white mice that was ill. He was wearing plus-fours and heavy brown boots: he disappeared in the
direction of the mice; then he came back, white-faced, the deed
done, wearing those heavy boots. There was something caustic
and exasperated about him, as though he knew his life had
taken the wrong turning. With the encouragement of his father-
in-law, my grandfather, my father had also entered Lloyd's,
where he became a successful underwriter. He could have been
a singer, for he had a good voice and was musical. People came
regularly to our house to sing, and Michael Tippett, then a
music student, used to conduct. Once my father played over the
telephone to his eldest sister, who was a pianist, one of Louis
Armstrong's early records. She said, 'Why doesn't that man clear
his throat?'

My paternal grandfather was an architect, a gentle, un-
ambitious man; my paternal grandmother was the opposite. She
had a Napoleonic nose and drove her family into successful
careers or marriages. My father was born in a Queen Anne house
in Chiswick, now a laundry. The family never had any money,
and seems to have become worse off rather than better. My
maternal grandfather's elder brother, Frank Mackinnon, was a
Lord of Appeal. I have heard he was a 'great judge', who
tended to sleep in court. He was an authority on Jane Austen. He
had a heart attack in court, and, just before he died, he said to
my grandfather: 'It's a silly business.' My father's elder brother,

Humfrey, became a general. My origins were thus solidly middle class.

My father and mother cared what people thought, and liked us boys to make a good impression; my father liked us to say 'sir' to the right people, to wash for lunch, and, when we wore ties, to tie them well. We went to church now and again, but never regularly; my father liked it for the singing.

My mother brought us up in an enlightened way, but perhaps relied more on what she thought, theoretically, was good for us rather than on what she felt: in this she was 'modern'. Brains and spinach figured strongly in the nursery diet. Or she said: 'Don't you like fat? You *are* funny. Come on, eat it up. It's lovely.' I was soon refusing to eat any meat, living instead on cheese, lentils and nut cutlets.

As a girl my mother had pushed one of her younger sisters down a chalkpit in a pram, and used to pull the same sister over a grand piano by her pigtails. Later my mother grew more conformist. She was never very academic at school. But she and my grandmother had been much influenced by the headmistress of the last boarding-school she was at. 'Girls,' the headmistress had said, 'should always wear low heels.' When my father married my mother, the low heels vanished. Unlike my father, my mother was unmusical: when there was a good record on the gramophone, she was likely to say, 'That's a low plane,' or, 'What's that screaming?'

At five or six years of age, when being bathed, I was forever asking my mother to tell me why some men and boys were circumcised and some were not. She told me that circumcision was good when you went to hot or sandy countries, which Englishmen often did, because it prevented dust and sand getting caught up in the wrong place. I asked her to tell me all this constantly, because it gave me a mild thrill. At last she said: 'That's quite enough of that.'

At about this time I found the blue-enamelled key to a tap: it was shaped like a small cigar, and had a square hole in the middle which fitted the tap. Late at night in the bathroom I tied one end of a piece of string to this key and the other end to my cock, from which the key dangled, a fair weight: strange sport.

When I was excited or pleased by something, a painting, or other object (even an idea), I used to stretch out my hands above it and quiver my fingers like insects' wings, as though casting a spell, and I was unaware of what was going on about me. My mother took me as a small child to doctors and psychiatrists, who prescribed calcium pills and quiet. One of the doctors or psychiatrists was a woman, sensible, businesslike, and unforgettably repellent.

My brother Adrian was born when I was nearly six. Just before his birth Peter and I were sent to stay with our grandparents at Crockham Hill. We were *sensibly* prepared for the event. In Westerham we bought tin trumpets and when we heard about the new brother we blew them out of the window of the house at Crockham Hill, pointing them towards Edenbridge and the valley below. Our governess conducted this operation. We went to see Adrian when he was a day or two old, lying in our mother's bed; then we were taken to a local point-to-point. My mother tried hard to give my father the daughter he longed for; but she produced him four sons, the youngest, Andrew, being born five years after Adrian. My mother now and again told me I was supposed to have been a daughter. 'Oh, why weren't you a girl?' she used to ask me.

Soon after Adrian was born my parents set about selling our house near Edenbridge. Peter and I were told never to show ourselves when prospective buyers were touring the house. But once Peter, determined to be helpful, appeared just as a couple were leaving. 'Have you seen the water in the cellar?' he asked them. 'It's two feet deep.'

We moved to a William-and-Mary house at Blechingley, in Surrey. Though officially the Manor House, it was not the poshest in Blechingley, there being also a 'Court' and a tall, square Inigo Jones house, both of which were larger.

The Manor House had about forty acres of land, including an open space known to some locals as 'the Park' and to others as 'Thomas Land': this was in parts hilly, with many oaks and elms, several chestnuts, two vast rabbit warrens as porous as ant-hills, and a marsh. Thousands of rabbits sat before their holes on summer evenings or lolloped about, their white tails bobbing. Rooks and jackdaws nested in the oaks and elms, and the beaked white skeletons of rabbits lay in profusion in the soil. One of our delights was to shoot with an air rifle from a great distance at a herd of cows in Thomas Land: since they were so far off you had to aim many feet above them; and if you hit a cow, it pranced up and down on the spot with a sort of rocking motion, its tail stiff in the air. The marsh in Thomas Land was not large, but it contained snipe, which nested there every year: the vibrant drumming of the snipe, rolling across the sky, was an important sound of my childhood. But now the snipe have been gone many years, driven away by the poisons of the plastic age.

When we moved to the Manor House the tennis court, running from east to west, was in my father's eyes wrongly placed for the sun: he had oaks and elms uprooted so that the court could run from north to south; and he had perfect turf laid. My father was obsessional about that turf: when he returned from the City on fine evenings he would walk out in his dark suit on to the tennis court and pace up and down, up and down, minutely examining the velvet green. Then he might go indoors and open a bottle of port: he did this by heating up in the fire an instrument like a pair of giant pliers, with which he cut off the necks of the port bottles well below the cork.

At one end of a lawn by the tennis court there was a cricket net. Peter and I practised there constantly, with Jack Weeks, the gardener, occasionally bowling us left-arm spinners; or Denis Hamper, the gardening boy at that time, bowling us wild long-hops. I had a small flicker-book which showed moving pictures of Herbert Sutcliffe batting and Maurice Tate bowling: I would study them for hours. And I would bowl for a whole day by my-self in the hottest sunshine, following Tate's prescription for medium-pace outswingers: the arm brought over close to the ear and the first two fingers on either side of the ball's tilted seam. If this failed, you could rub one side of the ball in the dust, while shining the other with nose-grease; if the ball didn't swing then, there was something wrong.

Peter and I shared a bedroom overlooking the cobbled yard. In it was my 'museum', a glass-fronted cupboard, containing flint arrowheads, a piece of the first electric cable laid beneath the ocean mounted in a small glass case with a brass plaque, a rattle-snake's tail, a yellow-and-black model of a Fijian outrigger, a silver pistol from the *Egypt*, a ship with whose salvaging my grandfather was concerned, and pieces of resin or gum from the oldest tree in the world. Between Peter's bed and mine was a small chest containing a variety of birds' eggs in square compartments in a series of drawers which, small at the top of the chest, grew larger and larger towards the bottom. The chest and eggs were a Christmas present from my grandparents: the egg-shells had a particular dry smell, combined with that of mothballs. Peter, who loved birds, disapproved of the collecting of birds' eggs, and I agreed with him, though this collection may well have been a hundred years old. Slowly, by putting them in my bed, or throw-ing them, he broke every egg in the chest, the last, in the bottom drawer, being an ostrich egg, which took a good deal of smashing.

Sitting on my bed in our room, wearing a rough blue jersey, I sometimes had premonitions of death or illness at the age of thirty-three: 'If life is such an effort now,' I thought, 'how can I live long?'

I climbed on the roof of the Manor House, which was excel-lent for this purpose, and sat up on the gables in the evening sun, thinking: I thought how lucky and extraordinary it was that I was born English; and was not a beetle; or a stone.

I dug a tunnel by a circular thatched apple shed in the orchard and gave myself claustrophobia in it. It was satisfying to pick a crisp green apple from a tree and slice it with the worn blade of an old penknife. A memorable discovery, that seemed to con-tradict the laws of nature, was a hybrid tree, half-yew, half-holly, the one grafted to the other, and the tree flourishing.

An American family with three boys lived near us. The father was a big man with a face like a frog: he laughed a lot and loved chocolates. The mother was a resilient blonde who made scenes. Once they asked us to the cinema in a near-by town: for some reason my parents had to refuse. Then, at the last moment, we found we could go after all, but to a later performance. There was no time to let the Americans know that we could go; the film being good, we went by ourselves. As we were being shown to our seats, we saw our Americans friends sitting behind us. My father and mother panicked, and we all ducked down in the aisle behind the seats, in the hope that the Americans would not see us, since we felt our appearance at the film needed some explanation. As soon as we could, we all crawled, my father and mother leading, to another part of the cinema. The Americans must have spotted us.

When I was a little younger, perhaps seven, the American boys asked me to tea. Afterwards the eldest said there was a job to be done: he ordered us to follow him into the fruit nets, and insisted that we catch and wring the necks of the thrushes and blackbirds caught inside: if you pulled too hard, their heads came off. I rode home that evening, believing that I had done a terrible but necessary job, with some of the birds hanging from the handlebars of my bicycle. My father saw me, and was horrified and angry at the sight of the dead thrushes and blackbirds. He insisted that the next day I should cook the birds and eat them, though I never did.

My father was still frightening. When once I broke a large pane of the greenhouse with a cricket ball, I did not immediately tell him. When he noticed the hole, he asked me, 'Did you make that hole in the greenhouse?' I replied, 'Which hole? I didn't make one of them, no.' He took me out to the greenhouse, and I pointed out the hole I had not made: it was a tiny thing, almost out of sight at the back. 'I mean this big hole in the front,' said my father in a fierce voice. 'Did you make that?' I had to admit that I did. My father was furious, saying that I had 'split hairs' in a dishonest and lying fashion.

When I was a child I had the same nightmare over and over again. In this nightmare I was shut in some small container, in which I was going away, away, away, from the people and things I knew; it was terrifying. I would awake screaming and covered with sweat. It seemed to me that the container left from a place near the London Zoo. It was as though the container was in a rocket, a sort of Noah's Ark, that was leaving a destroyed world with animals from the Zoo to find another, habitable planet; and when this rocket was deep in space, I felt terrified and lost. Lost forever.

Peter went away to prep school. On the drive to the school the car halted at traffic lights: 'I wish those lights would stay red forever,' he said, his large brown eyes peering from beneath his enormous cap. After leaving him, my parents cried all the way home. A year later it was my turn to go to prep school. Before we left home, Peter and I, wearing our school uniforms, walked in the orchard, among the smells of autumn, saying good-bye to familiar things.

'Aren't you dreading it?' Peter asked me.

'No,' I said.

I smiled on arriving at the school. But at the last moment, when my mother left me in my dormitory, I cried and ran after her. I was homesick ever afterwards on going back to school.

Abinger Hill was an interesting prep school. When I first went there I could not tell the time, swim a length, or tie my tie on Sundays. When, five years later, I came to leave, this was the entry in the school magazine:

J. M. GALE. Came Sept., 1934. Prefect Sept., 1938. Head of School May, 1939. Cricket Colours, 1938, 1939 (Capt.). Rugger Colours, 1939. Soccer Colours, 1938 (Capt.). Boxing Cup, 1939. Cricket Improvement Cup, 1937. Golf Cup, 1939. Editor of the Magazine. Goes to Stowe.

It looked more impressive than it was. I cheated in the golf cup for a start, narrowly beating a boy called J. Farley, who is now a psychiatrist. I beat J. Farley in the final of the boxing cup, too, though he thought he won; he may have been right. The school authorities wanted me to win the boxing cup, since I was to be head boy, not a very authoritative one, the next term.

J. Farley was a tall, thin boy, with astonishingly thick and wiry brown hair and a freckled face with a snub nose. He had a habit of giggling with a low bubbling sound just as he was about to peel you off a sharp right-hander to the ribs. He could be quite awkward.

R. Farley, his elder brother, was an excellent mathematician, and had an odd spring-heeled walk. At home the Farley brothers owned a bull-nosed Morris as well as motor-bikes, and had been able to strip them down and decarbonize them from the age of nine or ten.

My locker number was nine. When I first went to the school locker number eight belonged to Edward Boyle, thirty years later Minister of Education, and number ten to Nicholas Mosley, Sir Oswald's eldest son, who was tall and thin, and stuttered. Both these boys were older than me. Edward Boyle was much as he seems to be today. He used to come last in the school obstacle race, and was called 'the Prime Minister'. Everyone liked him, and he was never discouraged. When we sat on our lockers for roll-call at the milk-break, he would pull up his shirt out of his corduroy shorts, grasp the fold of flesh round his navel, and empty into it the milk from his bottle. Then he would bend down his head and sup up the milk from his navel in noisy gulps. He must have had a supple spine. It was a good parlour trick, and earned him applause.

One day at the milk-break a master said, 'Hands up who pinched biscuits.' Three of us, feeling smug and honest, put up our hands. That evening, to our surprise, the headmaster, who had frightening eyes, beat us, trousers down, in his study with a long-handled clothes brush that had his initials on the back: it stung, and the initials came out blue and back-to-front on our bare bums: you could read them in the dormitory mirror 'G.J.K.H.'

During the Abyssinian War feelings ran high at the school between the supporters of Abyssinia and of Italy. So one week-end the headmaster said we could fight it out in the woods. The woods were large, and in them we built tree-houses, in which we were allowed to sleep on Saturday nights in summer, provided that the headmaster had inspected each tree-house and found it safe, with a headknocker to wake up each occupant if he began to sleep-walk. The tree-houses played a part in the tactics of the school's Abyssinian War. Nicholas Mosley was commander-in-chief of the Italians, with, among others, the sons of the family that controlled the *Yorkshire Post* – then supporting Abyssinia – as his lieutenants. Edward Boyle, though not a military man, was one of the Abyssinian leaders, and my elder brother, Peter, and I, supported him, as did more than half the school. After a day-long battle in the wood, we gave the Italians a tremendous thrashing, and went into supper triumphant. But the Italians did win a few local skirmishes, before admitting defeat. In one of these Edward Boyle himself was captured and tied to a tree.

At the age of thirteen at Abinger, my brother Peter was the finest boy athlete I have ever seen. He won everything, and his batting average in his last term was 94.2. He was marvellous with animals, particularly horses. He could do nothing academically. He had a brown-eyed, open face. I shall never forget the exasperation of one master, a hairy liberal, who was trying in vain to teach him.

Suddenly, beyond control, the master shouted to the class: 'On him, wolves!'

The class set on my brother.

Peter was impulsive. He threw a chamber-pot from a dormitory window one night: it landed at the feet of some parents visiting the school with a view to sending their son to it. Peter did a similar thing when he came home on embarkation-leave during the war: when he entered the house, Nelson Eddy was singing on the wireless: Peter heard the sound, picked up the wireless and hurled it with a great shout against a wall.

Once, when he was about twelve and I was ten or eleven, we were having tea in a café in London, and Peter said suddenly to the large, brown-stockinged waitress: 'Come on udders, give us some milko.' She said: 'Wait till I tell your mother.'

In our prep school cricket team Peter went in number four and I number six: often the rest of the team made about twenty between them, and we might make a stand of 130, Peter scoring by far the most. We were rather proud of ourselves. I remember one shot of mine in 1938: it was the first match of the season, against a school called Hillside: their captain bowled a medium-paced full-toss, outside the off-stump: I hit it square off the front foot past point for four: it went like butter. I have never hit a ball better. Cricket was worth playing for that shot alone.

Soccer was perhaps almost better than cricket, though less important to me: in soccer there were second chances, but in cricket, when batting, there were none. Rugger never seemed to me as good a game: it frightened me; strength and, because of the shape of the ball, chance, played too big a part. But I will never forget playing rugger on a foggy day, and drop-kicking the ball square between the posts and hearing the curious noise it made as it sailed into a thick mistletoe-like growth in a big lime tree beyond: a noise, as the leather struck the twigs, like the stubbing of human fingers.

Boxing I hated more than rugger. Before almost every annual boxing competition, I would go for a walk in the woods with the history master, a spruce, moustached man, and ask him if he thought I ought to go in for the competition or not. I always did go in for the boxing competition, mainly perhaps because I was small as a boy, and felt it. Boxing was so personal, defeat so direct, that I had to win. This master was more interested in spitting than in boxing: he organized gobbing competitions from dormitory windows.

Once I boxed a Hungarian boy. We had wrestled often, and were so evenly matched that our wrestling ended always in deadlock. Locked in combat with him, I could feel the strength of his inner eye. Being a Central European, he was more developed than me, and possibly stronger, but he knew little about boxing. We had sparred once, and I had never hit him, allowing him instead to rush me wildly; then I ducked so that he went over my shoulder. In the actual fight, instead of ducking, I hit him as hard as I could with both hands as he rushed in. This happened three times: each time he went down, and each time he got up. I couldn't bear it, and wished he would stay down. After that first round, which won me the fight, I never hit him again, but just kept him off with pushes. The next day he was sitting in the cricket pavilion, watching two of us play French cricket: he shook his head and grinned at me. Both my hands were sore from hitting him in that first round. At soccer he played inside-right in the school team, I played inside-left or left-wing. I always remember this boy's fast, rather blind, running, his legs going like pistons.

I learnt one thing about boxing: against an opponent your equal or better, set a pattern for some time, to lull him, then break it suddenly; but be patient, and never break the pattern too soon.

I, the smiler, the compromise choice, became head boy of that school, because my rivals for the job were too wild or rebellious.

'Take a change of air,' we prefects shouted to the boys that misbehaved at meals, whereupon they had to stand up on their benches. Once at lunchtime the headmaster ate a green caterpillar in a salad: he saw it, but munched on, laughing, setting an example. Although they were prefects, J. Farley and R. Hoare led riots: most notable was the bread riot, when the school's caterer, a large woman known as Piggy, was locked in the maths room, while boys chanted outside, 'We want better bread.'

R. Hoare's brother, Bam, once ate a fir-cone and violets, washed down with iodine. He had big nostrils.

The grounds of the school were large. On summer evenings we walked up from the swimming pool to supper in the main building: the path, dusty amid bracken, wound up a steep hill, past tall pines whose knotty roots lay exposed in the dust and pine needles. The light on those evenings seemed always red and fine, and a clear bell on a tower some way off sounded its notes across the valley. At the bottom of the valley was a rough track by a tarred fence: in hot weather the tar on the top rail of the fence formed blisters which I burst with my fingers. The school had an open-air dormitory in the pine woods and we slept in it in summer.

Parents of boys tended to be judged by their cars, and there was a standing competition, timed by stopwatch, to see whose father could drive the length of the drive fastest. A father with an ERA held the record.

One of my earliest memories of the school is again of J. Farley. At the age of eight we sat at the same table in the junior dining-room. One supper we hung our cocks out of our corduroy shorts as we sat at table and thought it funny. One of the north country youths who were waiters at the school saw us, and was shocked. A day or two later he was making the beds in an upstairs dormitory that was empty except for me. He came over to me.

'I saw what you were doing at table,' he said. 'Disgoosting.'

He forced me to sit on his knee, twisted my arm, and undid my fly buttons. His striped cotton jacket smelled sour.

'Disgoosting,' he repeated. 'You want to leave that thing alone.'

In the same way that I can still remember their handwriting, I can still remember which boys in the school were circumcised and which were not. The difference seemed important then, and there is no doubt we preferred those like ourselves. As a very junior boy I got a corking rise during weighing and measuring in a changing room, and had to go out, amid titters. Those changing-rooms had a particular smell of carbolic, scrubbed wood and well-used football vests: the smell would strike me with dread when I came back to school at the beginning of term and entered the swing-doors of the changing-rooms to hang up my cap and blazer.

The school's bootboy and handyman was called Bloggs, known as 'Judas' because he had swapped his girl-friend for the starting-handle of a Baby Austin. He was large, with a red face and curly yellow hair, and was very proud of his strength. At the beginning and the end of term, wearing a striped blue-and-white apron, he would struggle up and down stairs with the trunks, exclaiming, 'It's not heavy, but it's awkward.'

At Abinger fights organized by the senior boys were frequent. When two boys were wrestling, not too seriously, they would be surrounded by a group of older boys, who would encourage the wrestlers, so that for each contender the struggle became suddenly important and victory urgent. At the beginning of my first term I was wrestling a boy a little older than myself, called Nigel Pearson. Two Mond brothers, Nicholas Mosley, and several others, began to cheer us on: Nicholas Mosley supported Nigel Pearson. Nigel Pearson was stronger than me, but as we struggled on the floor I put the neck grip on him, and after what seemed a long time he succumbed to it. I had held it so desperately that I could scarcely force apart my hands locked round his neck. Thereafter I found that fighting brought favour, and I became known as a fighter, the gladiator and champion of a group of older boys, who issued challenges in my name, though I remained one of the smallest boys in the school. One boy I had to fight was

Michael King, son of Mr Cecil King, formerly head of the *Daily Mirror* group. Michael King was my age, though much larger, and like many large people, he was kind and gentle. He wore, with his brown corduroy shorts, curious knitted stockings of a coarser, darker, and thicker wool than the brown regulation stockings with their orange stripes: his stockings, obviously home-made, set him apart. Perhaps it was because of his stockings that I was ordered to fight him.

One evening at the end of term I was wrestling a boy three years older than me, whose father had a Lagonda and was to drown in the Atlantic during the war. I put the neck grip on him and he, stronger, put it on me.

The next morning I walked about with my head on one side, so that my ear touched my left shoulder.

'You've slept in a draught,' said the matron.

We went home for the holidays. A doctor, my future father-in-law, took one look at my neck and said: 'I can do nothing with that: take him to an osteopath at once.'

By now white-faced, and in some pain, with my head lying flat on my shoulder, I was driven to London. The osteopath, a wonderful man, a former professional footballer, had X-rays taken. Three days running I was driven, white-faced to London, with my head flat on my shoulder. The third day, the osteopath had me on a kind of rack, stretching my spine, his clever hands working, trying to unlock my vertebrae. Suddenly there was a marvellous click, and the colour came back to my face.

'That was the nearest thing to hanging I've ever seen,' the osteopath told my mother.

When I could get away from my role of fighter at school I used to go deep into the woods. My greatest find, with a friend, was a couple of young tawny owls, hissing and clicking their beaks in a hole in a white and hollow tree trunk in a swamp. They were light and downy and looked ancient. We took both, I am ashamed to say, and kept them in a sawpit on a diet of mice and insects. Sometimes we gave them mincemeat, which turned out wrong, since it lacked the pelt and bones owls need; after a bit my friend's owl went off colour, and the headmaster's brother-in-law, a doctor, diagnosed rickets, and prescribed brown bread and

Marmite, which the owls liked. The headmaster, who spent most of his spare time racing through the woods on the stripped-down chassis of a small, unsilenced Austin Seven, shot us rabbits for the owls. We also caught rats for them in traps like cages: to get a rat out of a cage, you were supposed first to drown it, by flinging the cage into a water butt: the rat, wide-eyed and desperate under water, struggled to get out. I tried to drown a rat only once.

On their improved diet, the owls grew, had flights in a barn, and watched cricket from our shoulders, swivelling their heads through a hundred and eighty degrees. In the same way that canaries have something to do with goldfish, so owls are in some way like cats; they are on the same wavelength. Ours had a feline independence: you could not order them about or train them to do something they did not want to do. Both owls screeched, but never hooted in captivity. Once, when we were taking them their evening meal, a full-grown tawny slid off the top of the saw-pit in the dusk: it may have been teaching them to hoot. Or, since owls seem to have a cat-like power, was it even possible that the mother owl had traced her young?

The appearance of that wild owl made us feel guilty about the life ours were leading. We started letting them fly in the open: at first they flopped on to walls about fifty yards off: then they took to staying out at night, and at last went off for good.

It seems now that those summers were always fine. The pine and beech woods near the school had turtle doves which made a wonderful noise in the morning and evening. Where are there turtle doves in southern England now?

At one point the school was burnt down. It happened during a cricket match between the staff and the school's chartered accountants. Francis Huxley discovered the fire in, I think, a linen cupboard. He ran out to the cricket field to give the alarm. We all ran back to the main building, now burning well. A waiter known as Jilly George was throwing top hats out of the head-master's study, and later had to be rescued when he was overcome by smoke.

After the fire we went home for several weeks while they put up temporary huts to replace the part of the school that had been burnt down. We all wondered who had started the fire. Rumour said it was a small boy, who, when we wore ties on Sundays instead of open-necked shirts, always tied the knot of his tie very small.

'It's not nice for small boys to have small knots in their ties,' the matron used to say to him, pulling him about as she re-tied his tie. 'Not nice.'

In winter the temporary huts they put up were heated by paraffin stoves. One evening someone pushed J. Farley, who stumbled and sat down on a stove: because the school uniform included those strangely thick corduroy shorts, he was not burnt. The incident gave him an idea. J. Farley started a cult of sitting on lighted paraffin stoves. Because of his thin build he could sit on a stove longer than any of us. I had an idea that part of his secret was ventilation: the corduroy shorts kept the heat out very well; but once it was in, it stayed in, trapped, and you were for it. I think J. Farley cut small air holes in his trousers; and it was almost certain he hardened his flesh with methylated spirits; others said he also used silk handkerchiefs. Whatever he did, you could not help admiring him.

I have never really enjoyed Shakespeare since those days at prep school, because, aged twelve, I had to play Titania in *A Midsummer Night's Dream*. And I have never played the piano since then, either: in one school concert my fingers became paralysed when I was playing Beethoven's Minuet in G, and there was laughter. Now, even the smell of a piano's keyboard makes me shudder.

When I left prep school I was still supple enough to chew my own toe nails. The assistant headmaster said: 'You'll get through life, Johnny, with that smile of yours.' Etc., etc.

At home in winter we tobogganed: this usually meant barrelling down the North Downs on a piece of bent-up corrugated iron. Nothing could rival corrugated iron for all-round performance; it was the prop of English winter sportsmen, although not everyone would admit its excellence. Many were gripped by a strange snobbery that prevented their deserting those wooden-framed Swiss toboggans or those sophisticated flyers adorned with steering bars. Yet a piece of corrugated iron, well handled, was hard to beat. Its strength lay in its versatility: on ice it roared and throbbed like a French diesel train; in deep snow it skimmed over the surface with a soothing hiss, beating a track for those that followed on narrow-shod models; even in slush and mud it gave a good account of itself, and that was what mattered most in England after eleven o'clock, on all but the snowiest of mornings.

We could usually find a piece of corrugated iron in the cellar or the stokehole; or we might pull a piece off the back of the potting shed. It had to be about eight feet by two, long enough to make a six-seater. When cleaned of rust and polished, it had to be skilfully bent into shape: upon this bending depended its speed. Jack Weeks, our gardener, was an artist at this: he knew exactly how to tap the hull with a copper mallet, never warping it or creating a jagged edge that might have slackened speed or wounded passengers. He had an eye for weather, too: before the first snowflake he would be in the woodshed, shaping the metal with deft blows. He made us a new toboggan every year, with as much care as a man building a boat for the Cambridge eight.

After a fall of snow, Jack Weeks, two Geordie maids called Maggie and Bella, my brothers and I would climb to the proving ground on the Downs. People wearing professional-looking skiing trousers and tasselled caps (brought from Alpine countries by cosmopolitan relations) would give us a scornful glance, before kicking off downhill, lying full-length on their shiny, massproduced models. But they seldom sneered after our monster, looking a bit like an inverted Nissen hut, had rumbled past once or twice in a spray of snow. Often they had to leap out of the way, for it was characteristic of corrugated iron, when at speed, that it was unstoppable and almost uncontrollable; it swept all before it. Many times did we look back up a hill, after a fast swoop, to see smaller toboggans scattered in our wake.

A trained crew could steer a little by swaying in unison – but this needed long practice and was not infallible. Braking or steering by one's feet was useless, and one could easily break a leg. Once launched, the best one could do was to hold tight and pray, relying upon weight and size for safe deliverance.

After the trial runs Jack Weeks would make adjustments and then he would go back to his work, seldom coming out again unless he heard that his piece of corrugated iron was unable to beat every toboggan on the hill. If we told him that there was a swifter rival, he would grumble about his having to waste time; but designer's pride always lured him out to help us. I cannot remember a year when his magic touch did not conquer the field. He was a genius.

Maggie and Bella were fine crew members. They weighed a good deal, and they had a low centre of gravity and a love of speed. They were invaluable for testing new runs through a fir wood, on the side of a slope so steep that it could almost have been called a cliff; for they were willing to take risks that might have frightened Stirling Moss; although I could never decide whether this was because of natural dare-devilry, or whether it was because they were almost blind without their glasses. Whatever the cause, the result was magnificent.

When we had found a good run we would bank it up with snow, and if the night was frosty we would water it. This produced a high-speed surface, hardening the ruts so that they became as stable as tramlines: it was then possible to toboggan in the dark, with the front passenger holding a torch. Our ambition was to have a mild smash on the last night of the winter holidays, so that we should not be fit to go back to school.

Despite our loyalty to corrugated iron, we went ski-ing in Austria and Switzerland several times as children. We stayed in warm Alpine hotels smelling of dry wood and mothballs. Tiny boys in breeches snaked downhill to the exasperation of stumbling English visitors. The guides were curly-headed men with high complexions and unsettling charm who had made good from a peasant background where the cows lived in winter under the same roof as the farmer and his family. Their breathtaking trousers vanished crisp and straight into impregnable ski-boots. They waltzed expertly with visiting Englishwomen, who were much affected by their virile simplicity. In the evenings the younger guides gave exhibitions of *schuhplattler*, slapping their hairy thighs and chamois-leather shorts with fearful cries. I remember the heavy food and the pumping rhythm of the hotel bands. One night a small, dark conjurer and his large blonde assistant did something odd with a white dove, a pin, and cigarettes. I won a small silver ski in a handicap slalom, and nearly killed myself tobogganing down an almost vertical slope: as I rolled over and over, the snow-capped onion on top of the village church circled in the sky. Peter locked me in a hotel cupboard, which crashed to the ground as I was trying to escape. Our sponges froze, and splintered into pieces on the floor of our room. At Saalbach, in the Tyrol, in the winter of 1937, just before the *Anschluss*, Austrian Nazis wearing swastikas drove up to our hotel for lunch: one imitated Hitler, and had the same moustache. My aunt, Aline Mackinnon, for long a Liberal candidate, was beginning her work for bringing Jews and other refugees to England from Vienna.

My bedroom at home looked towards the north, over the yard and a tall hedge, cut like the turrets of a castle, over the kitchen garden, bounded on the west by an old wall, to a thick line of trees, pine, ash, oak and chestnut, beyond which lay a shallow lake that had once held trout, but was now too muddy, and covered with water lilies. The kitchen garden had a rich, almost black soil, and was traversed by a smooth earth path that was black, slippery and in parts mossy. Once, turning a sharp corner of that path on my bicycle, I skidded sideways and stopped, putting down my feet: the front mudguard, turning sharply, had cut my knee and removed from it a wart, which it had sliced off cleanly. The wart never grew again; yet, if warts are removed deliberately, consciously, and in cold blood, they often do grow again, and even spread. But it seems that if you can uproot them unawares, take them by surprise, as you must a limpet on a rock, and as my mudguard did, they go for good. Have warts a life and a consciousness of their own?

The kitchen garden had frames of marrows and melons. In one corner, by the wall, by dark laurel bushes, and a great chestnut wound about with creepers as thick as ropes, was an old woodshed: I liked to watch another gardening boy, Alf Kettle, splitting logs and kindling-wood with axe and curved chopper.

46

I love to watch people doing things well, with spare movements: making beds, cleaning shoes, cementing bricks.

I used to go with Alf Kettle, in his free time, into Thomas Land, where we would thrash golf balls from one crest to another with ancient clubs. On Sundays Alf and his mates would let me sit with them inside the hollow trunk of a fallen elm, and I would listen to their conversation about girls and what to do to them, pretending I knew it all.

Lying in bed in my room in late spring, I could look up into the branches of a great oak, feathered with pale green, and see in the shape of the branches the faces of men. Always at this time of year, just before dark, a big tawny owl would sit up in the oak, motionless, though mobbed by sparrows and chinking blackbirds.

Although the lake below our garden was too muddy and covered with too many water lilies to hold trout any more, the shallow stream that ran from it through a withy bed was, in spring, full of fat, spawning roach that you could touch with your hand. There was an island on the lake, and when a little older I used to visit it in a canoe. I embarked from the low branch of a tree that stretched out over the water and was often the perch of a kingfisher. When paddling I used to dream; at one of these moments in the canoe I was first able to have some conception, for myself, of eternity, and, worse, of nothing; it was a frightening concept, tending, I was once told, to madness. At these times I used to think: 'No one has lived this moment before me.'

On the far shore of the lake was a wide lawn running up to the Court, an Elizabethan pile, with a long drive of flint pebbles and a huge garden run wild and full of neo-Grecian urns. The daughter of the family that lived at the Court was a good friend, brown-haired, with a lisp from faintly protruding teeth; she is now a nun. We played hide-and-seek and rescue in the garden of the Court, and once I fell from the top of a yew tree, my fall being broken by its branches. Some winters we skated on the lake, and at night they played the gramophone and shone the headlights of cars upon the ice as we glided arm-in-arm. The clear ice of a lake is better than the ice of any rink; it was marvellous to race upon the ice, speeding up by running on the saw-edged points of your skates, and then stopping suddenly by turning and grating sideways, the body straining at a steep angle, and the skates cutting a spray of powdered ice.

In summer we went haymaking in our paddock, beyond the run of Peter's chickens, which laid the brownest eggs. Peter became fascinated by chickens, and later on made a couple of precocious girls help him clean them out, the girls teetering on high heels, their nails gleaming carmine, their faces white with rage and powder. I once saw these chickens turn with hysterical ferocity upon a frog that hopped into their run. Haymaking in the paddock meant the smell of drying grass, grass almost brittle and a dull green like that of a cigar; and it meant the feel of chaff, prickly under your shirt against a sweaty back. Once a thunderstorm caught us while we were haymaking, a flash of lightning and clap of thunder coming simultaneously overhead: then, after drought, it began to rain great drops on dry earth, and there was a marvellous smell of the earth drinking rain. At the bottom of the paddock was a tall wellingtonia, like something from the redwoods of California, with a fibrous, maroon bark easily sliced by a knife.

Over a stile, beyond the paddock, was a field full of cowpats, which I never minded, even if I trod in one with bare feet, for a cowpat is innocent. At the far edge of the cowpat field was the brown water of Martin's Pond, in which we caught roach and perch: the roach, silver and diamond-scaled, with dough; the perch, brown-marked, deep-bodied, with worms. We bought our hooks and split-shot leads from the paper-shop in the village, and they were effective: a posh family, complete with chauffeur done up deadly, turned up at the pond one Sunday, and had no luck all day with their expensive rods and chromium reels, while we were hauling in silver wrigglers by the dozen. Oak and hazel bushes grew on the banks of the pond, the hazels giving excellent cover for fishermen as well as providing nuts which, when picked with the shell still a little soft and green, had a creamy taste. Cowpats and hoof-marks descended through reeking mud to the water's edge: the water was thick and brown, except when caught, full of golden particles, in a ray of sunlight. On the east bank, the flat, white trunk of an oak that had fallen years before showed just above the surface; the trunk is there, unchanged, today. Once our model steamboat stuck in the reeds at the south end of Martin's Pond, and Andrew's nurse, a fine, hefty girl, swam out to retrieve it. I was astonished by her splendid, massive body.

We went every year to Warbarrow Bay in Dorset. At first we took the rectory cottage in Tyneham, a small village just inland from Warbarrow, a place of autumnal smells and grey stone cottages. In the rectory cottage we were bathed, aged three or four, in a brown tin bath with a high back. In the evening my father used to fish for bass off the beach at Warbarrow, where a stream joined the sea. His reel whined as he cast out over the breakers towards the sunset. One night after we had gone to bed he brought in to us by candlelight a gleaming silver bass that he had caught half an hour before.

After a time we took a house at Warbarrow itself each year: it was called Sheepleaze, and it stood on the cliff overlooking the sea and the blue hull of Portland Bill fifteen miles away across the water to the west. Constable painted a water-colour from this spot, which my father bought. The house was built of light grey Portland stone like granite, in which some kind of crystal glinted: the floors were of scrubbed white deal with rush mats; the sheets of the beds were rough and smelled of lavender; there were oil lamps. We ate mackerel straight out of the sea; breakfasts were of fried eggs and bacon, toast and bitter marmalade. In this house I was as happy as I have ever been. Each year my father ordered a barrel of rough cider, which came by train to Wareham, where we fetched it from the goods yard. In the evening my father tapped the barrel with Jack Miller, an old fisherman, the king of Warbarrow and its four or five cottages. Jack Miller would drain his glass, ruffle my hair, and say, 'You'm a rum young bugger, bain't 'um?' The cider barrel lived on a stand in the coal-hole near the outside lavatory: here there was always the smell of cider, dripping into the coal, mingled with the smell of tarred coal-sacks.

Most of the day, when he was not at sea lobster-potting, Jack Miller sat outside his cottage, which was built on a mound reinforced with stones, just above the beach. He wore a dark blue ribbed hat like a deerstalker without a peak; a thick, almost wiry, blue jersey over his great stomach; thick trousers speckled brown and grey; and black seaboots. His face was oblong and imperious, the nose and mouth stubborn, the blue eyes amused. He sat with his great brown hands crossed over a stick in his lap. Now and again he would rub a long scar on the back of his left hand, and say, 'Look y'ere: I did that with a conger-'ook thirty year ago: went poisoned.' He told stories of people and the sea, of a wedding party drowned in the tidal race of St Albans Head fifty years before.

The Millers were a great family strong about that coast, and most lived into their nineties. Jack's brother, Tom, a silent man with a round, salt-burnt face beneath a blue cap, brown eyes, small round nose, and fluffy beard from ear to ear, helped Jack with the fishing: Jack sat like an emperor in the stern of the boat, giving instructions, while Tom rowed, saying nothing. Jack was married to Miggie, a tiny woman with dark hair, who prepared us lobsters: Miggie, who seemed old to me, had a mother called Granny who lived behind the cottage in a small shed. Tom Miller was unmarried and lived in a tall, gaunt house, with a sister.

Warbarrow Bay was a wide crescent of sand and shingle facing west. The high cliffs to the north were of chalk, engrained with dark patches; and above them stood a Roman camp covered with short sea-grass. The high chalk cliffs sloped down south to crumbling sandstone and red clay; and then, beyond Jack Miller's cottage and the two boathouses with their granite slip-ways, a rocky knob of hill rose suddenly three hundred feet, with a sharp point running from its base out to sea. This was the Tout, whose north wall of sloping rock formed the south wing of Warbarrow Bay, facing the high chalk cliffs of the northern wing. It was a steep climb up the Tout, but rewarding. At the summit, embedded in rock, was a large metal ring that had secured a cannon in the Napoleonic wars. The wind up here was always fresh, with gulls motionless upon it. To the east you could see inland beyond Tyneham to woods and smooth hills of a silvery green slashed with chalk scars; also to the east, but nearer, rose Gad Cliff, far higher than the Tout, with a brown and rust-coloured overhang that was the home of ravens and peregrine falcons; at the foot of Gad Cliff, among high rocks, was a smugglers' hole. Fishing below this cliff from a boat at night you might get into a hundred-pound conger eel; and there were fine pollock. Beyond Gad, farther east, the coast became grey and slaty by Kimmeridge, before turning light again towards St Albans Head, where the tidal rip showed white and foaming on the calmest day. Near by, between Gad Cliff and the Tout, was a high-walled cove, sprinkled with caves, in which we over-turned rocks in pools to catch small elusive eels for bait. Immediately below the Tout, running out westward, was the rocky point where the sea was always choppy. You could catch heavy green-and-orange wrasse from the point; and it was good to stand upon it in a gale, with the spray flying up a hundred feet. Looking north from the Tout you saw below the Roman camp the high chalk cliffs which, as they ran westwards, suddenly fell vertically, and then rose again: this gap was the tiny current-streaked bay of Arish Mell, where a footman from Lulworth Castle, later burnt, had drowned. The cliffs that rose again west of Arish Mell flew a red flag when tanks were firing on the Army range just inland, and it was dangerous then to fish from a boat in the waters opposite. Going farther west, the cliffs sloped down, changing to a sandy, grassy point that turned and ran south into the sea to end in three red triangular rocks facing Warbarrow Bay: these were Mupes Rocks, and from the Tout the next thing you could see beyond them was Portland. Below a hill not far from Tyneham was a Queen Anne house with peacocks on the lawns. Just inland, between Warbarrow and Tyneham, and below the sloping backside of Gad Cliff, where we found mushrooms, was a thick wood, the trees nearest the sea stunted by the salt wind; through the wood ran a stream which you crossed by stepping stones; the trees were full of wood-pigeons, and there was honeysuckle.

We went barefoot at Warbarrow; and we stayed barefoot when we went into Corfe or Swanage to buy locally-made sausages or fishing tackle; our bare feet made a muffled slapping on the pavement. When we went back to school at the end of the holidays it was strange to change from bare feet to woollen stockings and heavy shoes.

We had a broad fishing-boat at Warbarrow. Oars on this coast did not fit into rowlocks: they had great wooden half-moons fastened to them just below the handgrips, and each half-moon had a hole in it, through which fitted a metal spike on each side of the boat, where rowlocks normally would have been; and these metal spikes, on which the half-moons of the oars fitted, were the axes on which the oars swung. A single man could rest his oars and attend to his fishing without any risk of his fixed oars slipping overboard, which they might have done with rowlocks. We used to go out most evenings trolling for mackerel and pollock with the small eels as bait. We came in after dark, with phosphorescence blazing off the bows of the boat in the black water and our hands numb with cold; on landing we pulled the heavy boat by hand up the steep shingle beach, then went in for supper, which would include the fish we had just caught.

Some days the mackerel came right inshore in shoals after whitebait: they were crazed, and would take even the bare hook, so that we hauled them in ceaselessly, silver, green and blue, zig-zagged with black, jumping and flipping in the bottom of the boat.

Conger-trotting was the best of all. A conger trot was a stout cord nightline with twenty-four six-inch hooks, twenty-four marker corks, and two boulders on the sea bottom at either end of the trot, to secure it. We baited each hook with a mackerel's head. We shot the conger trot at night, trying to avoid tangles as the hooks went down. Next morning, before breakfast, we ran out on to the cliff in front of Sheepleaze and scanned the sea for a sign of the marker corks: if the corks were bunched together, as they sometimes were, it meant we had on something big; for the corks to be bunched, the fish had to be strong enough to move the two boulders to which the conger trot was secured at either end. When the corks were bunched, we gulped breakfast, and then rowed out to them. My father, or, later, Peter, would haul in the trot with drops of water sparkling off the slimy cord: first, one of the boulders came up; then, one by one, the hooks, with the remaining mackerel heads sucked blind and white by sea lice. My father would begin to strain.

'Yes,' he would say, 'we've got something here.'

We were tense: there was always the chance of losing him. It might be a conger, coming up, thrashing and twisting, its black shape distorted by the depth of the water, until, suddenly, my father would call for the gaff, and the flat, black head would come over the gunwale, to be dealt a terrible blow with a wooden bar. A big conger would always twist the trot into a cold, wet tangle. We always took the best conger steaks to Charlie Miller, who was said to be at least ninety when I first knew him. Whether he was the cousin or the uncle of Jack I never learnt. He lived with a little white-haired wife in a small dark cottage in a dip near a spinney just behind the bay. He had been a fisherman. Though usually in a chair when we visited him, he was tall and magnificent with a straight nose and black eyes. Conger steak had firm white flesh: Charlie Miller said it was the best food there was.

Before breakfast one sunny morning we saw from the cliff that the corks of the conger trot were bunched closer than they had ever been before. We didn't wait for breakfast, but went straight out in the boat. My father started to haul in the trot, which seemed light.

'He's gone,' he said. 'Whatever he was.'

We felt awful. My father went on hauling, and I leant over the side of the boat and trailed my fingers in the water, which was green and transparent, since the bottom here was sand. Suddenly, in the shadow right under the boat, I saw him: a grey shape, like a torpedo, undulating.

'Look out,' I said. 'He's still there, just below us.'

By this time he was almost breaking surface and I reached down with the gaff, which caught the monster's lips; at this, the shark regurgitated the hook, which shot out, free. Peter and my father came forward and grabbed the gaff, and, as we heaved, the shark's head broke surface and he began to fight. We got him in somehow, a wonderful shape, gleaming dully, with an oily, rancid smell: a blue shark, though really more slaty-grey than blue, and white underneath, with five gills.

'He can't have been on long,' said my father. 'He was dazed, and didn't have time to get angry.'

I rowed in with my bare feet well away from those teeth, but pressing on the shark's back, which was as rough as sandpaper.

Jack Miller was pleased with us: the shark lay near his seat for weeks, and, to his delight, it upset visitors.

My father continued his bass-fishing from the shore; one afternoon, below the chalk cliffs to the north of the bay, a whirlwind picked him off a rock on which he was standing with his rod, then dropped him; he had seen it approaching across the water as a small waterspout, never imagining it would come straight at him. In the same spot a torpedo came ashore in grey weather and, in some way connected with the event, there was the smell of carbide. A destroyer hove-to in the bay, and a naval party rowed ashore in a whaler to retrieve the torpedo, which at last they did, with great difficulty in the high seas, by tying a rope to the evil grey cigar, and towing it off.

Two prisoners on the run from Guernsey or Jersey landed one night in a tall white motor-boat they had stolen: next morning the abandoned boat lay on the beach, and we walked round and round it, hoping the two escaped prisoners would not be caught, yet alarmed at the thought of them. Another visitor was a middle-aged man who was paddling round Britain in a blue canvas canoe and eating, as an advertisement, only bananas: he had yellow hair, a muscular brick-red upper body, and he seemed a bit simple. He paddled off in the evening sun towards Portland. What might he be doing today?

Peter and I got one shark by ourselves: he did the work. Andrew's nurse, the girl who had swum out to rescue our model steamboat from the reeds in Martin's Pond, came out with us in the boat. Jack Miller praised us to our faces for the first time: 'You'm real young buggers.' Andrew's nurse was a delight to Peter and me. She wore a pink-and-white uniform, a starched white cap on her fair hair, and black stockings. We liked to be chased by her and, preferably, caught. She was a strong passionate creature and smelled of soap. She supervised our supper in the nursery at home in the Manor House, and let us smoke, though I hated smoking. She told us we chewed our nails because we needed something.

'What do we need?'

'Oh, you'll find out one day, I expect.'

She loved Andrew in a tigerish way. I fell in love with her when I was twelve or thirteen. I was then sleeping in a tent outside Sheepleaze because there were so many people staying in the house. After supper I used to go into the crowded, smoky sitting-room and ask her to come and say good night to me. People must have noticed my devotion. In the tent, when she bent over the bed to kiss me good night, I kept her there as long as I could in the dark. I used to dream about her strong marbled body.

From the age of eleven or twelve I had been allowed to paddle my canoe out as far as the point running westwards from the Tout. The canoe was in some ways like an Eskimo's *kayak*, and would slice through heavy seas. Paddling far out alone, with the sharp bow driving through the chop of the waves and spray flying in my face, I would think of Andrew's nurse, and paddle faster; then, at last, I would hold the dripping paddle still across the moulding of the cockpit and glide, thinking. I would remember how I, too, like Andrew's nurse, had once swum in Martin's Pond, which seemed far away, but clear: I had swum in the muddy water, reeking of fish, and had let myself sink till my feet touched the unpleasant caressing mud and, occasionally, a hostile stick; down I had gone, my feet sinking through the mud, until at last the mud grew firm and my feet would sink no farther; then it had been time to kick up from the mud, firm at last, to the surface, to burst up into the crackling sunlight.

One fine Sunday morning we stopped playing tip-and-run on the grass in front of Sheepleaze (I had been imitating Alf Gover's wound-up bowling action) and went in to listen on the wireless to Mr Chamberlain declaring war. We went out again in the sun, and stood about talking and laughing: it was war, we were going to see life. Out beyond the bay, a destroyer from Portland was manoeuvring at speed, heeling over steeply as she turned.

Part Two

My mother returned to Warbarrow after helping with the evacuees at Blechingley. Her talk was mainly of sandbags. She was to drive me to Stowe, near Buckingham, for my first term. We drove across the fields from Warbarrow, and at the top of a hill looked back: Sheepleaze lay far off, tiny, a square stone with chimneys; the Tout sat there unmoved; the sun shone on the bay; the three Mupes Rocks were visible, but not Portland Bill. It was the best place in the world.

We went through Winchester and spent the night in some dowdy country hotel where there was staying another new boy to Stowe, Anthony Quinton, who seemed remarkably large. We reached Buckingham for lunch in the White Harte: a small, lively boy with bright eyes and a hoarse voice was jumping and gesturing at a near-by table, sometimes, when he spotted a friend, clasping his hands above his head like a victorious boxer. This turned out to be Wayland Young. My grey flannel suit, the school uniform, felt prickly. Outside the school grounds we had to wear absurd grey hats, half-way between sombreros and trilbies, which we doffed to masters and parents. Before going to Stowe, I had believed that all public school boys were witty, cynical, and enlightened, leading dazzling lives. After a day or two at Stowe I was astonished that anything could be so dull: the school seemed a lifeless cardboard sham in comparison with my prep school.

'Is this all there is to it?' I kept asking R. Hoare and J. de Bois Shrosbree, who were new boys with me. Peregrine Worsthorne, who had also been at the same prep school, had by then been at Stowe for a year or two, and I wondered how he stood it.

The buildings were impressive, if you like the mock-classical. Stowe had been the home of the Dukes of Buckingham, and the great grey-brown pillars, so they said, were hollow and filled with rubble and refuse: a jerry-builder's job. Some of the houses were new, and so was the chapel, of whitish stone, with gilt and light-coloured wood, in which we were encouraged to bellow the hymns – a rare and happy release. Many parents had, like mine, sent their sons to Stowe in the belief that it was a modern school; but though then little more than fifteen years old, the place had a good deal of absurd ritual, which made it in some respects a sort of fake Eton.

Art had been a pleasure at my prep school; at Stowe it was frowned on, though the art school was large and modern and the art master and his wife intelligent and charming, both Canadians. Art had a vaguely homosexual connotation; games were the thing. I have heard that in comparison with many other public schools Stowe was enlightened: the others must have been odd.

Being a clean-limbed little conformist, with fair hair and a smiling face, I learnt to shun the art school and to concentrate on games, which had always been my strongest line; things were not too difficult. Because of my attitude, I was soon made what was called a 'settler', a sort of junior monitor, whose job was to make life unbearable for boys of his own age and younger in the house who were not yet senior enough to have a study but spent most of their spare time in a large communal room dominated by a billiard table, and with the names of old boys in gold on the walls. A settler's main task was to punish boys that sat on radiators: Sir Miles Thomas's son was an habitual offender, and must have hated me, with good reason. I disliked being in authority, but to be officious seemed the easiest line. In those days Sir Miles Thomas was Mr Thomas, and worked for Lord Nuffield: he used to turn up at Stowe before chapel on Sundays with his head peeping out of a utility Morris armoured car, and he would bellow at us excitedly.

When I was there Stowe had something over six hundred boys divided among, I think, eight houses. The then headmaster, J. F. Roxburgh, who made Stowe successful, was at heart a kind and intelligent man, though a snob. One house would specialize in the sons of black marketeers; one in the sons of self-made men from Lancashire; yet another in the nobility. It was Roxburgh that decided which category a new boy came under and, I understood, to which house the boy should be sent. He was always kind and gracious to me, but since I was neither an aristocrat nor a scholar, I was scarcely to his taste. He took each form once a week, and addressed even the smallest boys as 'gentlemen'. After beating a boy he would sometimes offer him sherry.

New boys had their voices tested and, to my horror, they found I had a good one. A portly bouncy little man with curling silver hair and a tenor voice, a typical case of hyperthyroid, had somehow got in on these proceedings, though not a music master, and also new to the school. After the testing of our voices, the little silver-haired man called out, 'Which is Gale? Will he stay behind, please?' The little man then went to the piano and again tested my voice, which, alas, apparently hit the right notes once more in a piercing treble. This must have been a case of mistaken identity, since neither I nor anyone else had known I could sing. The outcome of all this was that I was more or less forced into the school's madrigal society, which had about eight members: I had to sing a duet, 'Two Little Maids from School are We', with a boy called Donald Duck, in front of a large audience in the school library; and was chosen to play a female lead in *The Pirates of Penzance*. In the end I got out of this torture by insisting to a music mistress known as 'the Radish' that my voice was breaking, which was an obvious lie.

The bouncy little silver-haired man began to have an affair with an acquaintance of mine, an eccentric curly-haired boy of about my age, who claimed to me that he had seduced the little man, and not vice versa. The boy came back giggling with presents: cuff-links, a dagger, a forty-year-old gold-embossed school belt. In the end the boy's elder brother got to hear of the affair and sought the advice of another boy (who later became a Trappist monk), who told the excellent history tutor, who told Roxburgh, who quietly asked the little silver-haired man to leave, which he did, taking with him his puzzled little wife.

At about this time my housemaster gave me what was popularly known as a 'balls talk'. This consisted of his sitting with fierce unease on the edge of a chair in his study: the talk, ostensibly about the facts of life (which, living in the country, I had known from the age of five or six), went something like this: 'Gale, you are now at an age when you may, er, get certain *feelings*. When you do . . .' And here there was a big pause. 'When you do have these, er, *feelings*, the thing to do . . .' Another pause. 'Is, er, er, nothing.' We also had a talk on the same theme from the school doctor, Dr Bostock, who prescribed long runs.

Girls, who seemed to me hopelessly remote, inflamed my thoughts. Much of my time was filled with pin-ups and fruitless pillow-bashing, with thoughts, above all, of Jane Russell. Every boy must know the despairing joys of masturbation, and no doubt it is as harmless as we are always told. Yet at fourteen or fifteen, desire and sexuality are stronger than they will ever be again, and it is sad that most people never benefit from it. If we could have had normal sexual experience early, we might have been better and kinder lovers in later life. And for this reason I regret my unfruitful adolescence.

Certainly boys had affairs with each other at Stowe: how widespread this was I was never sure. If they were discovered, expulsion usually followed. Several older boys had crushes on me, since they thought me a pretty little fellow: I was ill-at-ease, frowned haughtily, and was considered stuck-up. One of my admirers was a lord, and this rather appealed to my snobbish instincts at the time. He was in the colts' cricket team, I was in the junior colts, and we glanced at each other, discreetly, in the bus when travelling to and from away-matches. He had wavy fair hair and was distinguished, though girlish. We were in different houses, and never actually spoke to each other.

In my first year at Stowe I was given my house colours when our house team won the cricket cup. In the second innings, on a crumbling wicket, and facing 1st XI bowlers, I was in a stand with the captain of the house team, who made well over a hundred: I made no more than ten, but stayed in over an hour, giving my partner time to make a lot of runs. We had frequent conferences half-way down the pitch. The award of house colours meant that I would wear a special tie and coloured scarf when still very junior: my lordly admirer liked this so much that he sent me a Christmas card at home that year, somewhat to my embarrassment. Yet I was pleased by his admiration in a way that was distinctly feminine. He was killed with the RAF at the age of eighteen or nineteen.

I had a passion for one boy at Stowe: he had fair hair, dark skin, brown eyes, and a body of real beauty. To see him in a shower after a game of rugger was a delight. He loved animals, and often had a grass snake in his shirt, which I found a bit much. I had heard that his morals were not impeccable; he was very discreet. I was a fastidious prude. We did not know each other well. He and I were walking from our house to the main building one summer evening.

'Hmm,' he said, looking at his watch. 'Half an hour before supper. Half an hour to kill.' He hummed a tune, not well.

I had an idea he was dangling a bait.

'Yes,' I said. 'We are a bit early. Stupid.' I paused. 'By the way,' I said. 'I'm going to be a monitor next term.'

'Are you?' he said, feigning surprise.

That was the extent of our romance.

We were sitting in our form room at the beginning of one term waiting for our new form master, who suddenly entered; he came in rolling slightly and mounted the rostrum: a short immensely powerful figure, with short thick arms and a powerful head with curly brown hair and large brown protruding eyes: he was, in his own words, ' a sort of gigantic dwarf'. He spoke in a soft lisping voice that was in some contrast to his appearance. His name was John Davenport. His job was to get us through School Certificate. Though he now insists that he did not have a beard at that time, I always see him with one, large and bushy: to me he has always resembled Henry VIII, and he has never changed. Though John Davenport has had his enemies, we loved him from the start. His quiet fastidious voice could silence a black marketeer's toughest son by the charm and interest of what it said. He taught us history. We were not a clever form; officially we were classed as dull, even stupid. John gave us an interest in learning: he treated us as adults, and threw into his teaching fascinating anecdotal asides: it was disgraceful, he told us, that the Dauphin's jailers had taught the boy to masturbate, 'though this in itself is not necessarily a bad thing'. Here he was touching

63

on something that concerned us all. He taught us about Palmerston, Jack Johnson and Hollywood. At a tense moment in the last war, he wondered whether Japanese battleships could get through the Suez Canal, which, he thought, might be crucial. He woke us up.

He was never a jingo, but he taught us to love England, and advised us what to drink. Only once did I hear him raise his voice as a schoolmaster, and that was when the friend with whom I first shared a study insisted on reading *The Fountain* by Charles Morgan in John's history lectures.

'But he's not a good writer,' John Davenport protested.

'I disagree,' said my friend, who continued reading.

On summer evenings John Davenport played Bartok on the piano in his room, which infuriated my housemaster, who said it kept the boys awake. John taught at Stowe for only a year. We never forgot him.

Some of the more disreputable boys at Stowe wore camel-hair overcoats; one was a hero, reputed to have a child. The eldest of the three American boys we had known at Blechingley got into trouble at Stowe when he was discovered with a maid in a cereal cupboard. Sir Miles Thomas's son used to meet a large dark-eyed maid of great charm in an alley between the squash and fives courts. When I became a monitor and then a prefect I was told to spy on him from the roof of a classroom in order to catch him red-handed. I used to cough or make rustling noises so that he and the maid had time to get away.

'It's not right that boy taking advantage of a simple little serving maid, a skivvy,' said my housemaster. He retired and a new housemaster took his place: 'You're too naïve, too straightforward in these matters, Gale,' said the new housemaster, when I failed to catch boys with maids. 'Life is not straightforward: you must be cunning.'

I went in first-wicket-down for the school's cricket XI, but seldom came off because I was too nervous. My bowling was more successful. In athletics I won my heat in the mile and was second in the half-mile, but cut the finals of both, since I hate running, and knew I could win neither. I was a prefect, one of ten or eleven. I passed Higher Certificate, an examination that was no use to me, though preparation for it ruined my last year at school. I was a prig. At the age of seventeen I left Stowe and became a recruit at the Guards Depot, Caterham.

Up to this time, the great moment of the war for me had been the summer holidays of 1940, which we spent at Blechingley, below the North Downs. Peter and I lay on the tennis court that hot September, watching through field-glasses dog-fights and vapour trails high in the blue. Denis Hamper, the gardening boy, who was about to join the Navy, marked up the score of German aircraft destroyed on the wall of the green room above the stables where he kept the chicken-feed. A Spitfire with a bullet in its engine made a forced landing in a near-by field, just avoiding posts stuck into the ground to discourage Germans from landing there by glider or parachute. Denis had taken the Spitfire's pilot to telephone. 'He was a tall chap,' Denis told us. 'Didn't give a damn.'

My mother continued as usual to organize for us our annual holiday cricket matches. We had in our side an excellent left-arm fast bowler called Buster Baynes, then a much better player than several boys who later played first-class cricket. The most important match was always against the team of a cousin of ours called Locket. Some Toynbees, whom we had known all our lives, took part in some of these holiday matches: they were Harrovians, not great cricketers, and wore spiral-patterned caps and, below their white flannels, brown shoes with studs. We continued playing one match at Limpsfield during an air raid in which two Spitfires shot down a Junkers 88 near us. Several mothers set upon my mother furiously because she did not stop the match, which we won.

One Sunday, German bombers in formation, with escorting fighters overhead, sailed over our house towards London, later returning in formation by the same route. As we looked up at those lovely silver shapes flying south, a single Hurricane fighter dived through the German formation, shot down an escorting Messerschmitt 110, from which the pilot baled out, his parachute a small puff in the sky, and then rolled low over our house.

The next day a friend of my father came for a drink in the evening. He was a lugubrious man. He and my father were discussing a London evening paper, which had a large picture on the front page showing three German aircraft falling in flames in the same patch of sky.

'I happen to know that picture's a fake,' said my father's friend, who seemed despondent about the way the Battle of Britain was going.

That night a Heinkel III was shot down at Caterham, not far off. The next morning my brother Adrian, then aged nine, and I bicycled to the spot. We found the Heinkel, which had come down on a row of pink-and-cream bungalows, where it had burned, though it was not completely destroyed. 'This belongs to *them*,' we thought. There was that bitter, intoxicating smell common to all aircraft; and there was also the smell of acid and of burning. While we were examining the wreckage, the air raid sirens moaned and we took cover. Then, while most people, including the sentries that had been guarding the aircraft, were in the air raid shelters, we crept out and returned to the Heinkel, pulling from the wreckage a large piece of metal, which I took to be aluminium. It was a good souvenir. I tied it behind my bike, and rode home with Adrian, with the long piece of metal clattering on the road behind us. That evening we showed the piece of Heinkel to our father. I remember it well: we were in the garden room, which had large windows and a tiled floor.

'Hullo,' I said, turning the metal over. 'What's this? There's some writing.'

We read the words clearly printed on the piece of Heinkel: MADE IN BIRMINGHAM.

My father laughed: 'That's what war's all about,' he said.

Soon afterwards we went to live for a time at Bucklebury in Berkshire. In the spring holidays Peter and I travelled up to London by train for cricket coaching at Lord's. Jim Sims, of Middlesex, was the bowling coach: a kind man. 'You want to get up in the morning,' he used to say to me. Sir Pelham Warner told Peter that his bowling action was like the great O'Reilly's. We reached Lord's one morning after a big raid: an unexploded landmine lay deep in a hole in the road outside; the roof of the indoor bowling nets was shattered.

At Bucklebury we had a pony, which we rode in and out of

the oaks in an avenue. I was never good with horses. Once, un-harnessing the pony from the trap, I daydreamed and, unaware of what I was doing, took off the pony's blinkers too soon, before she was free of the shafts: seeing the trap behind, she bolted down a long wide path bisecting the kitchen garden: at the bottom of the path was a large greenhouse: I watched, fascinated. With the trap rattling and bouncing behind her, the pony went faster and faster; at the last moment she saw the greenhouse and swerved violently: the trap left the ground and swung sideways through the greenhouse, demolishing it; the pony was unharmed. I walked up to the house and found several people, including my father, who was on leave, drinking in the drawing-room.

'Jenny's galloped the trap through the greenhouse,' I said. They laughed. Slowly it dawned on them it was true.

Our gardener at Bucklebury was a simple man with a peg-legged walk, a stiff shuffle. We understood that a gamekeeper had shot him up the behind when he was poaching: because of this he could not ride his bicycle round corners, since, had he done so, he would have slipped from the saddle. We provided him with a .410 and my mother rationed his cartridges: he kept down grey squirrels and pigeons, and claimed he never missed. He shot our smoke-blue Persian cat.

At Bucklebury Peter and I shot a good deal of game: partridge, pheasant, and hares. In winter we trudged the sodden turnip and cabbage fields. There were also rabbits and pigeons in abundance. To shoot a tough old wood pigeon on the wing seemed a feat then, usually possible only when he was flying away from the gun, and you could shoot him calmly from behind, so that the shot went up his tail and not head-on against the armour of his breast feathers. Because we were shooting for the pot, to supplement wartime rations, we more often shot pigeons without sporting scruple when they were sitting in the trees. In the evenings Peter would go into one long dark wood of fir and larch, and I would go into another a mile off. Each waited, still: when a flock of pigeons landed with a clatter in the tops of the firs and looked about sharp-eyed, with bobbing heads, we would hope to get two birds with each barrel, since they roosted close: with the shots, the whole flock would fly to the other wood, and so we would keep them moving, and bring home enough for a stew. It was a good time to think, waiting on fine evenings in the dark fir woods. Often at this time Lancaster and Halifax bombers would go streaming out to bomb Germany: they would still be climbing as they went over us, staggering heavily-laden into the darkening sky.

It was at Bucklebury, at the age of fifteen or sixteen, that I first heard of syphilis when reading *Reader's Digest* up an oak tree and sipping beer from a bottle: an article was full of it. 'What's syphilis?' I shouted down to a friend who was about to join the Navy. I was upset by what he told me, and still am.

On one of his leaves my father took Peter and me over to Blechingley. It was a fine day in August. We visited the house of a doctor, whose family we had known for years: he was then in the RAF, but also, at that time, on leave. We walked through the house and out on to the lawn in the bright sun. The doctor's son and daughter were sunbathing: she was about thirteen, dark, with long black hair and large, serious eyes in a small face that had a strong chin and a chipped, upturned nose; her skin was olive, sunburnt with a tint that was almost green. Her name was Jill. She and I were opposites.

Peter followed my father into the Coldstream, and was commissioned. We were enemies in many ways until this moment: we had fought from the earliest days, often so bitterly that Adrian would run to my mother, crying, 'they're killing each other, they're killing each other, I know they are.' Only once did I beat Peter in a fight. Though by nature no fighter, he used to win because he was seventeen months older and stronger than me, and knew it, and I knew it, too. In the one fight I won he threw an axe at me and missed, and I gave him a left-hander, which demoralized him, before he could get his hands on me. I cannot remember the cause of a single one of our fights. We hated each other most of the time; yet we were very close.

In the summer holidays of 1943, before I went to the Guards Depot, I rode a lot. Then I got mumps, not badly. Andrew's former nurse came to stay: she was by this time a VAD, and almost as entrancing as ever, though my love for her was perhaps a little less passionate. She was a good person to talk to. We walked and rode together when I was recovering from mumps. She came into my room late one evening in a dressing-gown just as my mother was saying good night to me. She would have stayed after my mother had gone. But my mother called her out, rather peremptorily, I thought.

'Come on, we must leave him to sleep,' said my mother.

So I became a guardsman at seventeen and was worried that I had never slept with a girl. Somehow the thought of syphilis, nerves, the fear of bungling, and even the presence of a real live girl rather than a pin-up all combined to put off what should have been not too difficult. My mother, when we discussed the question, which was seldom, felt one should wait for the 'real thing' when one was married; my father, a little later, advised me to have as many affairs as possible and a late marriage.

Most of us wore our Home Guard uniforms in the train from Victoria to Caterham: the khaki prickled our legs. We had met on the platform, and were all public schoolboys, destined to be officers. A truck met us at the small station of Caterham. We entered the Depot by the Fox Gate, named after the pub there. We climbed from the truck and followed an old guardsman.

'You po – o – o – or buggers,' said guardsmen digging trenches, as we followed the old soldier in single file through a thin wet copse to the lines – rows of dark huts by an asphalt parade ground. Potential officers in the Coldstream and Irish Guards, we were in a Brigade squad in the Grenadier lines; future officers in the Brigade of Guards were then never trained by their own regiments, lest they returned later as officers and took their revenge on NCOs that had harassed them when they were recruits. On our first night at the depot there was a loud air raid; two Grenadier corporals hanged themselves with their braces; a guardsman bayoneted a friend in the latrines; and in our hut a boy called Hubert Doggart had a screaming nightmare. All night there were bright magnesium fires from incendiary bombs.

Next day an old trained soldier showed us how to fold our blankets in an exact square, a terrible feat. 'Do you understand it now?' he asked us. 'No,' I said. So he fixed me with an awful stare from a cold dark eye. When we wanted to pee, we stamped to attention and cried, 'Permission to fall out, trained soldier, please.' If this was granted, we turned right, with another stamp, and ran. Everything was at the double.

A grey-haired Captain in the Coldstream lectured us on regimental history, in a vague and rather charming manner. The Coldstream, he told us, was the oldest regiment of the Brigade of Guards. Its antecedents were Cromwellian, and as Colonel Monck's Regiment of Foot it took part in the campaign in Scotland, including the Battle of Dunbar on 3 September 1650. Later it was prominent in the Restoration of Charles II, and on 1 January 1660, on the orders of General Monck, the Regiment started from Coldstream to march on London.

Thomas Gumble, chaplain to General Monck, said: 'The Town of Coldstream because the General did it the honour to make it the place of his residence for some time, hath given title to a small company of men whom God made the instruments of Great Things, and though poor, yet honest as ever corrupt nature produced into the world, by the no dishonourable name of Cold-streamers.'

They shaped us with drill and polishing. Drill I loved: there was a beauty to it and a rhythm. A halt of precision by the whole squad gave real pleasure. A proper stamp of the foot did not jar the skull or drop the arches: it produced a singing click like that of a good iron shot at golf and a louder, more plocking sound than a stamp that was badly-timed and harmful. It was good to throw about a heavy rifle as though it were a stick and shine the woodwork with dark tan and spit. The toes of our boots were like glass; so were our cap-straps. I loved to polish leather: it was timing and rhythm here, too, as you polished, that brought up the cold gleam on the bird's-eye grain of the red or orange leather of the cap-strap. You could mix methylated spirits to the polish, but only a little, or the leather cracked: best was a bone or the handle of a tooth-brush, handled in a way that did not create friction and make the leather warm and the polish sticky, but, rather, stroked it fluently. To get that surface like a mirror's on the leather you had to get the rhythm right. It took hours of practice: the best time was in the latrines at night, as you sat among the poems: 'It's no good standing on the seat, the crabs in here can jump six feet.' Polishing here was a creative relaxation, for by day they chased us without cease.

'You dozy shower, you want to stop pulling your pudden,' the NCOs cried. 'At night people like you want to wear boxing gloves.'

The rumour about bromide in Army tea was always strong, and we recruits began to believe we could taste it. But a woman psychoanalyst, a princess, deflated this belief: 'The troops circulate unfounded rumours of sex-deadening bromide in the tea to relieve themselves of the complex, guilt-arousing challenge of sexual adventures.'

Constant chasing brought great hunger. Guardsmen, we understood, got extra rations because of their size; certainly the food was plentiful. There was a true giant among the Grenadier recruits, seven feet tall and twenty stone: his features were huge, dark, and square, and he had a great voice. He got twice the normal rations. Yet he would still say, 'Need all that, son?' And he would eye my plate. I did need it. When I joined the Depot I weighed less than nine stone; in the nine months it took to become an officer I put on another two stone and grew three inches.

One morning at breakfast at the Depot it was my turn to carry in the great metal containers of porridge to the mess-room tables; my studded boots slipped on the stone floor, and a gallon of porridge went over an old trained soldier, who sat there in a scalded fury, his head and shoulders thick with the grey, dripping mass, the livid eyes just visible. 'You young sod,' he spluttered. I shook burning porridge wildly from my fingers, which brought further cries of rage from guardsmen at the table.

After a few weeks at the Guards Depot, we were judged smart enough to be allowed out for the day one Sunday. The sergeant of the guard at the Fox Gate inspected us before he let us pass. It was early in the morning: wonderfully fine, with a slight haze and dewy frost. A horse pulling a baker's van clopped past with smoking nostrils. I walked through the outskirts of Caterham and then into the country, down silent lanes of an almost suffocating green with dew sparkling on the grass on the banks. A cock crowed. My family had moved from Bucklebury back to Blechingley, and it was to Blechingley that I was walking. At the top of White Hill, on the Downs, I turned off the road through a clump of ash and sycamore, to get a view of the valley where Blechingley lay: it was faintly blue and hazy in the early sun, and there were wraiths of smoke or mist lying above the green fields and the mauve clumps of elm. Scarcely a house was visible in all that blue, green, and mauve; it could have been England five hundred years before. As I looked I could just make out among the elms the house where our friends the American boys had lived before the war; beyond it rose the tall Elizabethan chimneys of the Court; and beyond them was the Manor House, just showing: home. Did it feel like home? It was an unforgettably lovely morning.

When the camp commandant, a one-eyed earl with a black patch, examined us at drill at the end of our time at the Depot, he cursed us, because we had been trained by the Grenadiers, and the earl was a Coldstreamer. We moved on to Pirbright, a hutted camp in the middle of rust-coloured Surrey bog sprinkled with firing ranges and surrounded by pine woods. It was a wilderness; yet Brookwood cemetery was only three miles off, and the Odeon of Woking not much farther. Here we were chased more ferociously than ever by virulent Scots Guards sergeants: they marched us so fast we thought we must fall over; we went on route marches, sometimes doubling ten miles in full equipment.

I bought a cheesecutter cap, permitted in the Scots Guards, but not in the Coldstream: it was a cap with lines stitched across a peak that fell so steeply it touched my nose and hid my eyes: an old guardsman set up the cap above the peak with half a brass button-stick so that the top of the cap above the Coldstream star curved up and almost backwards like a Prussian's. I was proud of my cheesecutter; but my father, a lieutenant-colonel in the Coldstream, was horrified. At Pirbright we got wet, cold and exhausted; we fired live ammunition on assault courses and wrestled with barbed wire below freezing-point at night; in our nostrils there was always the smell of rifle oil. We learnt to drive trucks and ride heavy khaki motor-bikes on roads and across country: afterwards we would treat our instructors to teas-and-wads in roadside caffs. There was something about driving a truck that was like riding a horse: the same rules applied. You gathered a truck, feeling it with your hands, in the same way that you gathered a horse before cantering. There was a satisfaction about changing gear with a crash gearbox, listening to the speed of the engine, to the note of the revs, and then flicking in the gear-lever: unmusical drivers crashed their gears and had no feel for the agony of metal. Yet you had to be a little brutal to ride a heavy motor-bike across country: you had to master it before the terrain, and then set it hard at the water, hump, marsh, or hillock. We wore great crash helmets, goggles, denims, and powerful dubbined boots.

At Pirbright we were exercised enormously, felt well, and, under that discipline, were free – a dangerous condition.

We went on to OCTU at Mons Barracks, Aldershot, already famous for Regimental Sergeant-Major Tibby Brittain, whose tuneful screaming carried three miles. Here we began to show the awful qualities of leadership. I got hopelessly lost when leading a compass march, but turned up somehow at the right place, and was thus considered promising. We had an exercise with assault boats at Runnymede on the Thames. We drilled our companions without mercy, and went on long runs on the ashen paths round Aldershot sewage farm.

Peter, a subaltern in the Coldstream, was on a draft for Italy. 'I'm not coming back,' he had told me. 'Don't worry.' He had laughed. I couldn't get a pass to see him the week-end before he left.

On one night exercise we carried the minimum of equipment and were ordered to share blankets when we slept: one blanket for two officer-cadets. It was a starry night. I dossed down with a friend, and we rolled against each other for warmth, and slept. We were on heathland near Liphook, peaty soil with heather, birch, and pine. We woke at dawn to find our arms round each other. He was a fair, attractive boy, strong and teddy-bearish, even catlike, fond of women, and, like me, of himself.

We went to Snowdonia for a battle course with live ammunition and forced marches in the mountains, doubling ten miles with Bren gun or two-inch mortar. I had just had 'flu. We assaulted positions on high and slaty ridges, firing from the hip, to the terror of the sheep. There was often wind, dark clouds overcame the sun, and we were soaked by rain and sleet. Mountain pools and lakes glinted under the changing sky. One night we slept in huts in a half-derelict quarry, near the cottage of a quarry-worker and his wife and daughter: the daughter spoke Welsh, and was a beautiful, wild-looking girl, with long black hair and blue eyes; she spoke to us, but was shy. In our company there was an officer-cadet called Levine, trying for a commission in a line regiment. He was ordered to command the company in one attack, muffed it slightly, and was reprimanded. As I lay in a firing position that day in marshy ground between the rocks, giving covering fire for an assault, the barrel of my Bren gun steaming, I thought of Levine, and wondered if his dark, Jewish looks were against him in the Army. He was a good, intelligent boy, very gentle. He never got his commission.

A few days after returning from Wales to Mons Barracks, I received an envelope with the Royal coat-of-arms on the back. Inside was a crisp piece of notepaper with a black crown on top above the words WINDSOR CASTLE. Below it said:

'The Master of the Household has received their Majesties' commands to invite O. C. J. M. Gale to a small Dance at Windsor Castle on Friday, 5th May 1944, at 9 p.m. Dress: Short jacket, black tie; Officers – uniform.

'This invitation must be presented on entry to the Castle.

'A reply is required.'

An officer-cadet in the Irish Guards, called McGrath, and Angus Sinclair, in the Scots Guards, son of the Air Minister, received similar invitations. The adjutant of Mons Barracks, a thin, ginger-haired Captain in the Irish Guards, who wore tall, glistening red field-boots, sent for us.

'You'll need a haircut,' the adjutant said. 'See you're spotless, of course. And carry a gold cigarette-case in the breast pocket of your battle-dress: always useful when the conversation dies.'

'I don't smoke, sir,' I said.

'Take a gold cigarette-case all the same,' replied the adjutant. 'And call the Queen and the Princesses "Ma'am".'

5 May came and we left for Windsor Castle in a fifteen-hundredweight truck: Captain Mark Bonham-Carter, Grenadier Guards, a recently-escaped prisoner-of-war, and at this time an

74

instructor at Mons Barracks, had charge of our party. He sat in front next to the driver. We drove up to the grey battlements of Windsor Castle, passed through a stone archway, halted, climbed out, and entered the Castle.

The 'small dance' seemed fair-sized to us. We found ourselves in a big room, with an orchestra below what was, I think, a large and curving window. It was brightly-lit, and there were almost certainly chandeliers. Rooms led off on either side of this big room, which was in effect the ballroom. The orchestra struck up. I had never danced in my life. I seized a young girl of about my own age, who turned out to be a lady-in-waiting: she was pretty, but frosty, in a pinkish dress. We said little; I bored her, and trod on her toes. The orchestra stopped playing. We stood together, saying nothing: I felt large and rustic; my shoes, which belonged to Peter, were too big, and turned up at the toes. I remembered the gold cigarette case that I had, with some difficulty, borrowed for the occasion.

'Have a cigarette?' I asked the little lady-in-waiting.

I wrestled with the button on the left-hand breast-pocket of my battle-dress, in which the cigarette-case bulged. I tugged out the case, which I had filled carefully before leaving Mons Barracks. I tried to open it; I struggled for what seemed a long time. Suddenly the elegant cigarette-case burst open, and cigarettes flew all over the floor, where people were again dancing. I went down on my hands and knees and grovelled for the cigarettes, some of which had been trodden on. I retrieved most of them, and stood up.

'Have a cigarette?' I again asked the young lady-in-waiting.

'I don't smoke,' she said.

'Nor do I,' I said.

I took refuge in one of the side-rooms, where I had a drink: the drinks were excellent; there was hock cup, most refreshing. The orchestra began to play 'Hands, Knees, and Boomps-a-Daisy', and I found myself taking part. The Queen (now the Queen Mother) enjoyed this very much, and several times our bottoms boomped. Later she sat on the arm of a chair, and talked to several of us; she laughed constantly; no doubt she guessed we felt out-of-place.

Princess Elizabeth and Princess Margaret wore brocadish dresses, and were surprisingly small, but comely. The face of King George VI was heavy with orange pancake make-up; his head was small. (I remembered my father telling me how he had tried on the King's cap in a cloakroom when the King had lunched at the headquarters of the Guards Armoured Division: the tiny cap was new and without blemish, and had perched like a toy on top of my father's head.)

Although I could not dance a step, it seemed absurd not to dance with the future Queen. After a few more drinks, I went up to her.

'May I have the honour of this dance, Ma'am?' I asked.

Princess Elizabeth consulted her card, which bore a serpentine list of names, and murmured that, for the next ten dances at least, she was taken.

'Perhaps later?' she said.

I had more drinks, felt well, and got jammed in a tiny lavatory with a general of Commandos. At two or three in the morning, feeling by now robust, I approached Princess Elizabeth again.

'Ma'am,' I said. 'I believe this is my dance.'

I put out my arms to her. Before I knew exactly what was happening, we were on the dance floor, and beginning to sway in the right direction. I realized I had had a lot to drink. We said nothing, but swayed and rocked to the music as best we could; I knew no steps. Happily it was a fox-trot, which made few demands. We said nothing for a long time. Was I perhaps leaning too heavily on my partner? The band played on.

At last Princess Elizabeth asked, 'Are you at Sand'ust?'

'No, Ma'am,' I replied. 'Mons Barracks.'

In the weeks before we were commissioned we went frequently to the regimental tailors in London to be measured and fitted for our uniforms: my tailors were in Hanover Square. There were, we were told, certain London hatters that could, and certain others that could not, make the regimental forage cap, which was dark blue, with a gold peak below the large Coldstream star; if you went to the wrong hatter it was disastrous.

The night before our passing-out parade there was a dance at Mons Barracks, very drunken. RSM Tibby Brittain was standing as sober as iron, with a pint tankard of whisky in his fist: people filled up the tankard all night. Some friends suggested I might get the Sword of Honour next day: I brushed aside the suggestion with false modesty; I was ambitious.

'You might have got the Sword, Mr Gale, sir, if you hadn't got the 'flu and missed some training,' said our company sergeant-major, an Irish guardsman. 'That's what did you in.'

I got really drunk that night for the first time: the world rocked and swayed, and I was terribly sick. Friends put me to bed. To get drunk was, it seemed to me, one of the things you had to do; to sleep with a girl, to fight in a battle and, if necessary, to kill a German were achievements to be added to that list.

Next day we paraded white-faced with hangovers. The Sword of Honour went to Hubert Doggart, who had screamed in his sleep that first night at the Depot. After the parade we dressed in our officers' uniforms, and looked at ourselves in the mirror: astonishing. Some of us were still only eighteen. We Coldstream ensigns were driven over in a truck to the officers' mess at Pirbright where we would command platoons in the training battalion. Our gold-peaked blue caps were down over our noses, our gloved hands held walking-sticks. When we climbed from the truck at Pirbright, guardsmen saluted us, and we acknowledged these salutes by touching the peaks of our caps nonchalantly.

Young officers at Pirbright were drilled and chased once more: 'Pick up your feet, Mr Gale, sir,' cried the drill-sergeants.

'Let's *have* you, gentlemen, please.'

We had to call all our fellow officers, even those more than twice our age, by their first names (only the commanding officer being called 'sir'): this was not always easy. We had each a personal servant, usually – in the training battalion – an old soldier: at first I was never able to treat my servant with anything but deference, and he, sensing this, became a tyrant. We trained our platoons and, in the officers' mess, ate too well and drank too much. But, because the Coldstream's antecedents were Cromwellian, we never had to drink the health of the King. We took turn as picquet officer, a tiresome duty, though it was a change to take a parade with a drummer: the picquet officer flicked his wrist to the drummer, whose drumming communicated the officer's orders to the troops, thus controlling the parade. On all these parades, the drill-sergeants, who were warrant officers next in seniority to the RSM, breathed down the guardsmen's necks in their anxiety to take names or put men under close arrest; drill-sergeants had to be restrained.

The invasion of Normandy came. The Coldstream's 5th Battalion had heavy casualties, particularly among platoon commanders: each of us hoped to be on every draft that was announced.

Every Saturday we went to parties in London: about most of us young officers in the Brigade of Guards there was an inexcusable arrogance: all other regiments were the 'Line mob', and their officers were 'charlies' to a man; we disregarded them if we could, patronized them if we could not. We considered it very 'charlie' to say 'phone' or 'give me a tinkle'. A senior officer, later in the Royal Household, was specific about the sort of language that 'wasn't on'. Here is a sample: 'I put on a pair of slacks, got out the old bus, buzzed up to town, and plucked a bird.' Yet because discipline in the Guards was strict, and the observance of it fell upon the NCOs, relations between officers and guardsmen were comparatively close and informal. But to see our behaviour at parties, no one might have guessed this. After almost every party we took girls to 'The Four Hundred' night-club; I could talk golf with the man on the door in a most patronizing manner. I preferred 'The New Nut House' in Regent Street, an orange-tinted dive full of coarse, floating blondes. Peter had made me a member before he left for Italy. He was now with the Coldstream's 2nd Battalion, and had gone up through Cassino: 'The men in grey,' he had written, 'are on the run.' 'Men in grey' had made my father laugh: 'Terrible,' he had said.

I got 'flu and tonsillitis and was laid up in bed at Blechingley. One morning the fat old village baker, a great gambling man, called up to my window. I stuck my head out to see him standing in the yard, feet apart, a large basket on his left arm.

'Mr John,' he shouted. 'It's your mother. She's had a terrible accident. All blood. We picked her up off the road and didn't recognize her. It was only because of the little dog we knew who it was.'

My mother, returning from taking Andrew, my youngest brother, to school on the back of her bicycle, had been knocked off her bike and badly hurt. Whoever hit her never stopped; they believed it was an Army lorry. They rushed her to hospital. She regained consciousness. In a few days she began to recover. But her face was terribly injured. One day a photograph of Peter, in uniform, fell from a shelf above her bed for no apparent reason.

'Oh,' laughed a brisk nurse. 'That's unlucky.'

At about this time fast, strange-sounding German aircraft began to crackle and snarl towards London, a pale blue flame streaming from their tails at night. The sound was infernal. A few days later the Government announced that this was the V1, the flying bomb. You heard the V1 coming a long way off: when it was about to dive and explode its engine cut: this was a tricky moment, the silence loud: then came the bang. I returned to Pirbright: a flying bomb just missed the mess. One wet afternoon I was out riding a motor-bike cross-country with a sergeant, and enjoying myself. A dispatch rider came out to us: the adjutant, Rupert Hart-Davis, wanted me. I returned to camp and reported to him.

'Oh, Johnny,' he said. 'They want you at home as soon as you can get there.'

I went home, through a London dark and apprehensive about the flying bombs. I knew why I was wanted. I went up to the room of my mother, who had just returned from hospital. My father and my Mackinnon grandparents were there. They handed me a telegram: Peter had been killed before Perugia just after his twentieth birthday, on the day his photograph had fallen from above my mother's bed in hospital. Everyone, I think, had expected this. When I returned to Pirbright, Rupert said: 'I'm sorry. But he was an awful ass, wasn't he? A nice one.' They buried Peter, who had loved birds, at Assisi.

They took out my tonsils in a military hospital in Aldershot, and the next day gave me toast. I returned to Pirbright, and longed to go to Normandy. One or two young officers of my vintage were beginning to do so; soon the first of them was missing in a minefield, presumed killed.

They sent me on a platoon commanders' course at the School of Infantry, Barnard Castle. An officer in the Irish Guards on the course took a dislike to me at first because I had a rather comfortable lining, bought at Herbert Johnson, Bond Street, in my tin hat. The course was exacting, and in the evenings I was often sick as a dog. But I commanded our company of officers in the night attack that was the climax of the course, and came out top, receiving an 'A': I returned, very smug, to Pirbright, preceded by a letter of commendation from the Brigadier commanding at Barnard Castle. I tried to get to a battalion at the front, but they made me an instructor commanding a demonstration platoon and teaching newly-commissioned officers night patrolling. A piratical sergeant, a policeman at Piccadilly Circus when last I saw him years later, blew off a young guardsman's foot accidentally with an explosive charge when simulating battle conditions. They kept me as an instructor, perhaps because I had had a brother killed in the regiment.

As the war was ending I crossed with a draft on a small boat to Ostend. Guardsmen blew up French letters and threw them overboard, to float like small airships on the grey waters of the Channel. We spent several days in a transit camp in a German forest. Then we passed through Goch, just destroyed so completely by Lancaster bombers that no one had tried to get the bodies from the rubble, crossed the Rhine, and drove up in trucks at night to join the Guards Armoured Division in North Germany. The Division was still fighting its old foe, the German Seventh Parachute Division. A red-haired subaltern in the Irish Guards, the son of a bishop, who had come out with us, was killed by a sniper within an hour of his joining his battalion. Most of us did not join battalions, but remained, frustrated, with a reserve company. We took German private cars from garages and, with the help of fitters, started them: it was looting. Many guardsmen were driving Mercedes; I had only an Opel. To visit the line, we drove up straight roads among pine woods, and passed neat German farms with broad roofs and wide eaves: split firewood was stacked immaculately outside. Once, accidentally, we drove through an outpost of armoured cars of the Household Cavalry, ahead of any English troops, and into enemy territory. Germans in isolated pockets fought to the end: some were Marines from Bremen and Hamburg, and among them were boys of fifteen and sixteen. A Gunners' Sherman tank was blown high into the air by a powerful sea-mine buried in the road.

We had heard of the concentration camps, and wished to see for ourselves. Two friends and I learnt of one at Soltau, just over-run by British troops, and we drove there. It was a lovely day. We came to the concentration camp at the edge of the town: there were dark huts behind high wire; and large pits full of grey flesh and bones; nothing lived. A party of SS men, watched by silent English sentries, was being made to load the remains of human beings into trucks and take them away for burial. In this party was a girl, also in SS uniform: she was beautiful, a blonde, almost birch-coloured. The sun shone, the earth breathed, and against a line of dark pine trees, this pale girl in the grey SS uniform carried the remains of what had been human beings and loaded them into trucks for burial. I felt then I could never make love to a German girl. I remember noticing that the trousers of the SS men had stitched creases: a practical device.

We went into Soltau and visited a military riding school immaculately kept: there were splendid white stallions. The sun shone into the whitewashed stables, hooves rang against the stone, and the friendly noses of horses showed at the grilles of their boxes.

The Guards Armoured Division advanced towards the Baltic: we heard on our Eighteen sets the last, drunken broadcast of Lord Haw-Haw, the traitor William Joyce, to whom we had so often listened on the wireless in England in the worst days of the war. Joyce was broadcasting from Hamburg, only a few miles ahead, as we closed in on the city; this last, drunken broadcast was in some way magnificent.

When the war ended, our artillery fired to herald it; some Merchant Navy men, just released from five years' captivity, swung on the chandeliers of our billet, and sang. We went to command platoons in the Coldstream's 5th Battalion, which moved on to the outskirts of an airfield at Cuxhaven, where we sat in the sun, fired captured weapons, rode large captured motor-bikes with sidecars, and continued to censor guardsmen's letters. With my platoon, I took a party of surrendered German para-chutists and set them to work carting and stacking captured ammunition: a fair, bronzed German sergeant-major had charge of the German party, and I rode with him in the cab as he drove a smoking German Ford truck towing a trailer to and from the ammunition dump. It seemed strange to be riding in a German Ford: commerce overrode ideology, principle, and war; and Ford of America could scarcely be the losers. 'No fraternization' was the order to the troops in Germany then; but I wanted to talk to those German parachutists. They often sang a song which stuck in my mind. It was, I learnt afterwards, a tune that bands played when German soldiers left their homes and marched to the station to take a train to the front in the First World War. Elvis Presley sang it years later as 'Wooden Heart'. It was, I now know, based on a theme by Beethoven.

One day I visited Heligoland aboard a captured German E-boat: the island was grey with the dust of bombardment. Quite often we drove into Cuxhaven and drank lager by the port in the cold evening sun. Once a German Marine shaded his eyes to watch a Mosquito taking off, and then shouted out something in a hoarse voice. Victory had made few of us cheerful; Germany in defeat was sad. The officers of one or two companies in our battalion succeeded in making contact with the officers of neighbouring Russian units, and had drinking parties. But within a week of the war's end the Russian authorities forbade this.

We moved farther inland, beyond Rotenburg. I walked in the pine woods in the evenings, and saw deer. Driving back from Rotenburg one wet day, my jeep skidded unaccountably on a straight road between dark woods: it occurred to me later that I had skidded at the spot where Captain Ian Liddell, v.c., of our battalion, had been mortally wounded by a German sniper a few days before the war ended; he did not live to know that he had won the V.C.

I took a truck and drove into the ruins of Hamburg to find beer for the company's canteen; it seemed then that Hamburg, buried beneath mountains of dust and rubble, could never live again. We found a brewery: an old drayman with waxed moustaches, wearing a leather apron and dark blue cap with a corded pattern, like the Kaiser incognito, rolled out the barrels for us.

The battalion moved south once more, through the shattered Ruhr, to Cologne. Just after the start of this journey, my platoon truck passed through a north German village at the very moment Himmler was captured there and took poison.

Our mess outside Cologne was in a large house that had belonged to a rich industrialist: there was a swimming bath; our bodies, for so long white under heavy khaki, became brown; an excellent string quartet played for us in the evenings. I drank too much, and spent one night lying soaked under a bush in a thunderstorm. I resented that I had not seen more of the war, and assumed a false and insufferable cockiness: indeed, one fine night a day or two after the war ended, some fellow officers had thrown me, almost unconscious with drink, into the branches of a pear tree.

From Cologne I took a week-end leave convoy to Brussels, with the circular outline of a French letter showing like a talisman in my wallet. On arrival in Brussels several of us rushed off to an *exhibition*: it ended with the fifty-second position, *la position Japonaise*, which involved one of the two kindly, naked, and middle-aged instructresses in standing on her hands. We all had a good laugh, but were, really, none the wiser. The whole performance took place in a stifling little apartment smelling faintly of old hot water bottles. In the end, a few hours before I had to leave Brussels and take the leave convoy back to Germany, I went in some desperation to the address of a classy brothel (its number in the street was 71), in a fashionable district, that had been highly recommended by older officers. The girls were, according to reports, charming, high-born enthusiasts, who loved English officers above all else. I stood in the drizzle on the steps outside number 71, wondering whether to knock. I must have stood there five minutes. In the end I didn't knock, but went away and had a plate of strawberries and cream, my first since 1939. I returned to Germany feeling I had thrown away the most important opportunity of my life and was a coward and a fool. Shortly

83

afterwards I heard that an officer in the Grenadiers had picked up a dose of clap in the same establishment.

Several of us volunteered for the war against Japan, and returned to England. I took with me a pair of sheets adorned with swastikas, several Luger automatics, and a Mauser parabellum, or machine-pistol, of dark blue, oiled steel, its wooden holster acting as the butt: years before I had seen Conrad Veidt, playing a spy in a war film, use just such a Mauser to blow up an ammunition dump behind the lines. An American sergeant in a division that had not seen action had offered to swop an armoured car for this parabellum. When I had taken these weapons from German prisoners, a tall, rather elderly German lieutenant, whom I disliked, had smiled and said: 'You will use these against the Russians? Good.' I had answered: 'No. The Russians are our friends. We shall use them against the Japanese.'

When we reached England, we found we were to take part in the assault on the Japanese mainland, but would first train for this briefly in Kentucky. We went on embarkation leave. It was almost dark when I got home. My family met me on the steps. My father's car, a 1936 Riley, with a pre-selector gearbox that whined, stood below. My father gave it to me. It was battleship-grey and it gleamed. The radiator was solid, and it shone. Inside there was red leather with a good smell. That car had clean and pleasing lines, and I was proud of it.

The 1945 General Election had taken place while I was in Germany. To my astonishment I found that my father welcomed the Labour victory. 'There might have been trouble if they hadn't got in,' he said. I never asked how he voted. My mother had always been a Liberal, because her sister, my aunt, had stood for Parliament as a Liberal before the war. I knew nothing of politics. All I knew was that fellow officers in the mess in Germany had said the election result, particularly Churchill's overthrow, was a disgrace. I was not old enough to vote.

Since her accident at the time of Peter's death in action in Italy, my mother had had several operations at the hands of a great plastic surgeon. He had built her a new nose with grafts from her hip. After one operation, the surgeon asked my father what he thought of the result. My father shrugged, and replied,

'Well, not so much, actually.' The surgeon knew Peter had just been killed, and for that operation he never charged.

The atom bomb fell on Hiroshima, Japan surrendered. I spent most of that leave with my family in Ireland, where we drank and played golf. There are few things like the singing click of a good iron shot off the springy fairway of a seaside course and the following hiss of the ball. Our hotel on the north-west coast was large and wooden, and owned by a Plymouth Brother who forbade public drinking: we drank in our bedrooms, twice as much as we would have done otherwise. Staying in the same hotel was a girl, then an officer in the WAAF, with whom as a child I had climbed on the cliffs at Warbarrow before the war. She was older than me, and had been fond of Peter. We danced together at night. And one day I took part with two men in a long and absurd swim, perhaps two miles, in a cold sea, largely to impress this girl. When I reached the shore, she ran down from the people waiting on the low cliff, and gave me a warm towel. That evening she said: 'Come to my room tonight: I want to give you something.' I went to her room and asked, 'What do you want to give me?' She laughed, and gave me a small present: I forget what it was.

Instead of going to Japan, we went to Palestine. On the troop-ship, a friend of mine burst open a bathroom door and found a captain scrubbing the back of a nurse. We saw Portuguese sardine boats, Gibraltar, and flying fish. After the troops had boxed, the brigadier organized a milling competition between the officers of the Welsh Guards and of the Coldstream: this meant one round apiece, flat out. I had to box a lieutenant in the Welsh Guards who had played rugger for the Army. He was strong, but luckily no boxer.

We landed at Haifa, and entered a camp in the area. The sun burnt us; we bathed from silver beaches; and guarded strategic points, including the stations of the unloved Palestine Police. At night there was that wonderful smell of the Middle East: a smell of dust, oranges, and mystery. My ambition was to buy a pair of suède desert boots, as worn by officers of the 8th Army in North Africa: suède scarcely existed in England then, and I longed to wear it. We soldiered on, sometimes cordoning settlements and searching for arms or terrorists. I think I can say that our Guards Brigade behaved well, and gave no sign of anti-semitism; though, from reports that reached us, the same could not be said of 6th Airborne in Tel Aviv. Terrorism, mainly by the Stern Gang and the Irgun Zvai Leumi, continued. They were brave, and almost always chose their targets with precision: their favourite was the Palestine Police; few of us doubted that the police used torture, or, at least, beat up suspects.

Often we were bored, spending too many nights guarding concrete police stations, peering down gleaming barrels at the barbed wire in the moonlight.

But a lovely Jewess worked in Barclays Bank in Haifa, and I could not keep my eyes off her when I cashed cheques. She was big and proud, wore yellow, and looked like an Egyptian goddess. One day as I walked to the door of the bank, she clopped out in front of me in high heels, and looked back. I followed her, but didn't dare speak to her. I followed her down the street and up some stairs into what turned out to be a sort of Jewish socialist lunch club: it was full of small men in overalls and enormous light-grey caps. My uniform felt out of place, and I retreated in confusion.

Soon afterwards I asked to be seconded to the Transjordan Frontier Force, a Beau Geste outfit that wore red cummerbunds and black kalpaks made of Persian lamb. I wanted to learn Arabic, the official language of the Force, which was a sort of private army belonging to the Colonial Office. The troops of the TJFF were Arabs, Druses, Shershans, and Circassians. The officers were British, with 'local officers' – mostly Arab, but one or two Jewish – serving under them. In the TJFF, English officers, it seemed, were considered abnormal unless they drank a bottle of gin a day and made passes at their drivers. The squadron I joined, with the rank of captain, was stationed at Safad, high in Galilee. I never knew quite what its job was: but on one or two nights people fired at us a bit from beyond our barbed wire perimeter. The drinking was enormous, and on most nights I had some trouble standing up; sometimes I went to sleep with my head in the soup. My squadron commander was a brave and clever man, now a diplomat. He taught me a lot. Sometimes he fought guests invited to the mess with a sabre; and once he had a duel, using full bottles of champagne, in which he nearly severed his wrist.

'You're a clean young Englishman,' he used to say to me. 'God help us! I can see your happy home: welcomes, a spaniel, an old nanny, and a faithful retainer in a green baize coat. You make me sick. Thucydides knew better.'

He would quote pages of Latin prose and verse; and then sing 'Cocaine Kate and Morphine Sue' at the top of his voice. This would go on till four in the morning, when he might decide to commit suicide; I then spent the time till breakfast hiding or unloading his shotgun. As the sun rose, we would wind up the gramophone and put on an old and scratchy record of Marlene Dietrich, singing, open another bottle of champagne, and feel better. At last the Arab servant, known, because of the cut of his beret, as 'the German Sailor', brought in a breakfast of eggs fried like leather.

If we were not up all night, I might go riding before breakfast. A *sais* found me a horse of my own, a large, ginger beast, handsome, but mad-looking. I decided to try him. A friend and I rode northwards in the morning sun; we cantered; we galloped. Then I found that nothing I knew would make my horse stop. I tried everything; useless. It was like John Gilpin. We galloped on and on down the white and dusty track, through gullies, with stones flying. We went through a village, scattering chickens and small brown children; the village elders shaded their eyes against the low morning sun to watch us pass. Then we leaped a road, and we were in Lebanon: my horse had galloped me across the frontier. At last he slowed down; he was foaming. I walked him back for a late breakfast, and told the *sais* what had happened. They found he was indeed mad, with an ulcer beneath his tongue.

The squadron moved to tall, square police forts on the Palestinian–Lebanese frontier, some way from any village, but quite near the spot where my horse had run away with me. The hills, covered with wiry, pale blue scrub, were brown and bony, and the sky seemed huge. One or two fellaheen in turbans and pantaloons ploughed small patches of thin and stony soil with wooden ploughs, which they steered between the rocks. I commanded a fort with a hundred men and two or three local officers, and lived and ate alone, tended by a fat, shabby Damascene called Abu Shem. Often at night I drank a bottle of gin by myself and wrote long and pointless letters in a large, inflexible hand. Near the fort was a deep ravine that scarcely saw the sun. In the afternoons, after the daily parades, inspections, and detailing of patrols, I walked along the top of the ravine, past the tall rocks, the blue and wiry scrub, and the occasional olive tree, silvery and twisted. I liked being by myself.

Abu Shem, grinning shamefacedly, asked to go on leave to Damascus, where his mother was ill or his sister was getting married. He borrowed five pounds from me, and went. Damascenes were famous backsliders in the Army, and I didn't expect to see him again: nor did I; no one cared. Another Arab, a good soldier, went on leave to kill his unmarried sister, who was pregnant: the local officer commanding his troop considered him an excellent boy.

I moved back to squadron headquarters, to share a mess with my mentor, the squadron commander, who had not cut down on his drinking. He was still singing 'Cocaine Kate and Morphine Sue'. One day we went into Haifa to arrange about stores. Afterwards we drank. After many hours, we left the bar, somewhere up on Mount Carmel, in search of another. The squadron commander paused in front of the long plate-glass window of a shop. At the side was a drive-in, lined with boulders. He walked with deliberation to a boulder, and picked it up; he walked back to the long shop window, and stood, like some caveman, looking in. Then he hurled the boulder through the plate-glass, and we ran. We ran towards a light above a door: we entered, and found ourselves in a sergeants' mess. The squadron commander stood on the bar and sang. We spent the few remaining hours of the night in an hotel: the squadron commander kept climbing out of the window and clinging to the gutter.

We returned to the squadron and found they were hunting bandits. The bandits shot one of our Arab troopers in the leg, and fled deeper into the hills. We came on a small village they had passed through recently. 'Do the men of the Frontier Force think we are birds to be caught in the hand?' the bandits had asked the villagers. In hospital the trooper's leg became infected, and they had to amputate it.

One of our few clear duties was to stop hashish smuggling, which was big business run by desperate men. The frontier we patrolled was long, and we never saw a smuggler. But the squadron commander and the local officers hatched a plot. By circuitous means, one local officer put the squadron commander in touch with a representative of the smugglers. The story the squadron commander told was that he was badly in debt and needed money quickly: if he, in his own truck, were to carry a big load of hashish the length of Palestine, from the Lebanese to the Egyptian border, what would the smugglers pay him? The smugglers answered: '£200.' The squadron commander believed that in this way he would learn the smugglers' secrets.

One morning he rose before dawn and waited in his truck on the frontier road: at the appointed hour four men with rifles slung over their shoulders came up suddenly through the steep and wiry scrub and dumped four large tins of hashish in the back of the squadron commander's truck, then they disappeared as swiftly as they had come. The squadron commander started on his journey. He left one tin, as ordered, in a gully under a bridge in Galilee, where a man was waiting; the three others he delivered to a house in a town near the Egyptian border. Then some smugglers took him out to lunch; one of them was a strong Arab elder with a snowy beard. They plied him with drink, to see if he talked; it was child's play to the squadron commander, and he did not. He returned to the squadron £200 richer, and the money went into squadron funds. But the smugglers never again asked him to run hashish for them, so we captured no one. Did they know the squadron commander's plans? Were they tipped off by the local officer? We never knew.

At least once a week we shot snipe and duck in the marshes of Lake Huleh, under the shadow of Mount Hermon in Syria, which always had snow on its summit. I found I shot best with a hangover, because I was then relaxed and unhurried. If you shot at the head of a flight of duck, you were bound to hit one: often it was a bird at the back that fell. Darting snipe withered in our fire. Our drivers and ragged Arab boys hired on the spot retrieved the birds. Snipe I had liked ever since they had drummed before the war above the marsh at Blechingley, where they no longer drum today. At about this time I gave up shooting for good. The sunsets over the marshes of Huleh were fine; and the white summit of Mount Hermon looked pink in the dying sun, when the land below was already dark.

I went on leave to England. I arrived home just before Christmas and went out to a party with my family. There was a French girl of seventeen there, auburn-haired, very feminine, and just a little plump. We danced the conga, and I remember my hands on her silken hips.

The next morning my younger brother, Adrian, was shooting with bow-and-arrow on the tennis court. A great elm, whose black winter silhouette I knew so well, rose above the bank against which the target stood. Adrian offered me his bow and three arrows. I stood more than the length of the tennis court from the target, and drew the bow, aiming high: the first arrow flew and landed with a 'pock' in the target: the two remaining arrows followed, 'pock', 'pock', making a close and quivering group of three.

A day or two later I received this letter.

I have no idea to begin my letter. Perhaps you will think I am very ill-bred but it is too difficult for me to look for a sentence not too respectuous and not too familiar – Dear John! I cannot say this because I do not know you very well.

I hope that you remember me and that you do not forget you have promised to see me in Paris.

I am afraid that you do not recognize who writes you because it seemes to me you do not know my name: you have met me at Missis Cohen's party: I wore a white dress and you walked on my feet because I danced so badly. You have taken my address and you have given me yours but you was really thinking something else because you have forgotten to say to me your name – happily, I am lucky and I have found.

I am afraid that you will think the French girls are very offinded because I would not have to write to you. I believe it is not in the English habits, but in France it is allowed to write to an almost unknown boy.

I hope you will answer me and you shall be able to say to me at what time you will go to Paris.

I send you all my good wishes for the new year and I beg your pardon for this bad letter.

Affectionately,

Michelle

I did not go through Paris on the way back to Palestine at the end of my leave: I had to return the way I had come. A truck from the squadron met me at Haifa. Half-way, we broke down late at night in the hills. A wildcat with a stump of tail ran across the road. The driver fiddled with the engine, then gave up. We dozed in the cab; it was cold. At one point, to warm myself, I walked up the road. Suddenly a ragged figure flew across in front of me, dropping something in the ditch as it ran. I shouted to it to stop, but it disappeared into thick bushes. I picked up what it had dropped in the ditch: it was a small sack of tobacco. The figure must have been a tobacco smuggler, one of many; they didn't make much of a living. When dawn broke the driver idly pulled the starter; the engine fired immediately. We drove back to the squadron. The squadron commander was not pleased we were late.

Not long afterwards I returned to 3rd Battalion Coldstream Guards in Tel Aviv. One day the Stern Gang blew up the station of the Palestine Police in the middle of our compound. Two or three of them foxed the guard by posing as electricians, with false papers. They drove in a van, parked it beside the police station, and then walked out of the camp and past the guard with a ladder over their shoulders, saying they were going to fix wires outside. There was a sharp, rather flat bang, and the police station disappeared. I ran to the spot. There was that particular smell of blasted masonry. We scrabbled with our hands in the rubble, and organized rescue parties. But hands picking at the rubble were the most effective.

We spent most of our time guarding something. One day I nearly severed a tendon near my ankle when clearing fields of fire with an axe. Talking to guardsmen at these times, I learnt a little about England. Most Coldstreamers were Yorkshire, Lancashire, or Geordie, with Londoners and Birmingham men among them.

'Have you ever known a widder with the rags on, Mr Gale, sir?' a Geordie, a former miner, once asked me, as we stood high up in a guard tower below the moon.

There was a guardsman in another platoon, not a very bright man, who reminded me of my brother, Peter. He had a moon-face and brown eyes. He got silently and paralytically drunk at a company party, and swayed about under the stars in the silver-darkness, with his mates jeering at him kindly. In some way this man moved me, yet I didn't know him. Compassion is a strange and rather awful thing, an impertinence, perhaps. Sometimes I have felt it for someone seen for a moment from a car and never seen again.

I went on leave to Cyprus. One day I swam from a golden beach towards a rock nearly a mile out to sea. I was then, I suppose, burnt and bleached in the best Aryan tradition. A delectable Jewish night-club dancer, whom I had seen perform, swam out in a friendly way after me, followed by her younger sister, aged about fifteen, who wore a white bikini and was one of the best-built girls I have ever seen (even better than her elder sister). The elder girl, who was nineteen, told the younger in kindly tones to swim back, which at last she did, grumbling, to the beach, where she lay down to the whistles of approving pink-skinned English soldiers.

The elder girl and I swam on, out to the rock, which we reached at last. She said she thought I was one of the many German prisoners of war in Cyprus at that time. I had to say I was not. We talked a bit and nothing happened. Nothing happened later when we met again. I have always blamed my middle-class public-school upbringing for that lack of initiative. An English working-class boy would not have faltered so lamentably.

It was, incidentally, almost as though the military authorities took all this for granted. Army guardrooms always had (and probably still do have) what were known as 'ET' (early treatment) rooms, which were equipped with various prophylactic devices: but these were for 'other ranks' who had been on the bash with girls outside camp and might have picked up an infection. There were no such facilities for officers, presumably because officers were not expected to go on the bash.

The battalion moved north to a camp built on red sand near Nathanya, a diamond town on the coast. It was a time when the British hanged several Jewish terrorists. As a reprisal, a commando of the Irgun Zvai Leumi kidnapped two British sergeants in Intelligence in Nathanya. Against orders, the sergeants had been sitting, unarmed, in a café. They should not have been out at all. We mounted a big operation to search for them. I was commanding a company. We searched the houses of Nathanya systematically: we searched villages and fruit plantations. In every house we apologized for intruding and were careful to do no damage. Some of the small homes were frowsty, with a sweet-sour smell, and full of bric-à-brac. In one a small elderly man and his wife cringed; I wished they wouldn't. The man kept rubbing his hands and rolling his eyes. 'I will give you the address of a wine shop, my cousin, in Hampstead,' he said. 'He has whisky, real whisky. It is difficult to get, I think, in England now.' He thrust on me a grubby piece of paper on which he had written the address of the wine merchant in Hampstead.

There was one house in particular in Nathanya in which we were told the sergeants might be hidden; my company searched it. We tapped the walls and floors and drilled holes; we found nothing. We never did find the sergeants: the only way to have done so would have been to use totalitarian methods and to pull the houses apart one by one.

They asked me to stay on in the Coldstream as a regular officer. But by now I knew it was not for me. My demobilization number was fifty-six. A great friend was being demobilized with me. The officers of the battalion gathered outside the mess to see us off.

'What's the betting they'll be blown up on the way to the station?' The officers shouted as they said good-bye. 'It would be typical.'

Our servants loaded our trunks into an open pick-up. We moved off, waving. Outside the camp we were to meet and lead to the station a small convoy of trucks taking men for demobilization from the other battalions of the Guards Brigade. Because we were late, and the train was soon, the convoy had started to move off slowly. We were not able to take up our position at the head of it, but slipped in as the second vehicle, behind a big Welsh Guards' three-tonner, which was leading. The road ran first by eucalyptus trees and then through sand-dunes. We passed the trees and were driving through the dunes when there was a bang: white smoke and dust rose by the three-tonner in front, which halted. It was a mine at the side of the road, probably one of those designed to resemble a kilometre stone, so that it should not be spotted. Far off in the dunes, a tiny figure in khaki shorts had sprung up and was running away towards a Jewish settlement, his short bow legs going like pistons. Something about the figure seemed familiar. He was the man that had detonated the mine. I ran forward to the three-tonner: the driver had blood running from his ears, and his truck was out of action. A sergeant took over the wheel, and I ordered another truck to hitch up and tow him on immediately, since just ahead on either side of the road were high banks and trees ideal for an ambush. Walking back to the pick-up I could not help feeling that it was just as well we had started late and had thus not been leading the convoy; for in comparison with the three-tonner, the open pick-up was fragile and exposed. We drove past the trees and the high banks without incident. I turned to Sergeant Wandless, a Yorkshireman fond of racing pigeons, who was sitting in the back of the pick-up with a Bren gun. He was also going to England to be demobilized.

'Why didn't you shoot that fellow who was running away through the dunes after letting off that mine?' I asked Sergeant Wandless.

'I'd have killed the poor little bugger, sir,' he replied. 'There would have been a court of inquiry. It would have delayed my demob.'

We caught the train travelling south to Port Said. Sitting in the train I realized who that running figure, the man that had tried to blow us up, had reminded me of as he fled away across the dunes: the way he ran had reminded me of the Hungarian boy whom I had wrestled and boxed at my prep school: it was a Central European's running.

In Port Said we waited several days, in a transit camp run by

German POWs, for a boat to England. While there I learnt that a friend of mine in the Grenadiers, leading a patrol in a wood near Nathanya, had found the two kidnapped Intelligence sergeants, for whom we had searched so long: their captors had hanged them inexpertly by pulling them up over the branches of a eucalyptus tree by ropes tied round their necks. Despite such incidents, I had become a Zionist, and a friend and I spent much of the time in Port Said arguing with an anti-semitic Padre, who grew purple in the face, as the three of us drank and gobbled prawn cocktails. At last a troopship, a hot, cramped, old Cunarder, took us back to England. A Grenadier captain I met on board said: 'Oh, hullo. I'd heard you were dead.' On a fine evening in the Mediterranean we hit a dolphin, whose blood stained the sea. And we saw blue mountains to the north. We docked at Liverpool on a hot evening: it was the famous summer of 1947, the Mersey ferries were crowded, and the troops cheered them.

A day or two later we left the demobilization centre at Woking, free men. I was twenty-one.

Part Three

Just after I returned home, my parents and some friends that lived near by gave a big dance in the friends' house. I wore my Coldstream 'blue', and played the officer-and-gentleman for the last time. During a waltz the pin came out of a man's wooden leg, which flew across the floor, scattering frothy girls. There were men in tails and white gloves. Jill, the doctor's daughter, whom I had seen sunbathing as a thirteen-year-old girl during the war, came to the dance. She was now a ballet dancer. Her hair was still long, strong, and black, and her eyes large and serious in a small face with a strong chin and a chipped, upturned nose. We danced together stiffly. She said very little. She was about to tour North America. That evening there were many girls more flashy.

I spent the first few days after leaving the Army in building a fence for the ponies near the tall wellingtonia in the paddock. I was never good with my hands: but the fence was not too bad, I thought. I was still sunburnt from Palestine, and I worked stripped to the waist, driving in raw wooden posts, and stretching the wire taut and securing it. It was something of an act. As I worked I talked to myself, and thought about my life.

We went to Connemara, and drank. For a moment I fell in love with a very young girl and to impress her at a party in our hotel, grabbed a well-known drunk who was dancing unsteadily, took him outside, and carried him upstairs: a typical example of my officiousness. Why could I have not left the poor drunk alone? Later, in the early hours of the morning, I went out walking under the watery moon and the outline of the hills: walking on a ridge separating two brackish lakes not far from the sea, I threw away all the coins in my pocket: they went curving up and away, and came down with a tight splut in the water. I thought I loved that young girl, but it came to nothing. I was a timid, cold virgin, and I loved no one but myself.

On returning from Ireland, I worked for a week in my father's underwriting box at Lloyd's. I understood little, except that I could not lead this life. 'Could you give me a scratch, sir?' brokers asked as they passed, touting risks involving astronomical figures. What did it all mean?

I failed to get into Oxford, so I went to the Sorbonne. I arrived in Paris on a pink evening.

In the taxi from the Gare du Nord to the Cité Universitaire, I took notes busily: the taking of notes, I had been told, was the sign of a literary man. 'Pink evening,' I wrote in my notebook. 'Fat taxi driver in cap: a character.' PARIS: streets full of people.' I peered from the cab earnestly. It was the last taxi I would be able to afford for some time.

In the Cité Universitaire, on the edge of a park, I lived in the Maison Franco-Britannique. My room had a buzzer that woke me in the mornings by buzzing and giving off blue sparks. I noted down those blue sparks in my notebook. Meals, very cheap and very bad, were in a huge self-service dining hall in the central building. It was the time of rationing – particularly of bread. For breakfast I had a large bowl of cocoa made with water. There were always large girls with moustaches and black dresses eating there. 'This is life,' I thought.

I felt I must keep fit, so I went swimming most days, even in winter, in a large indoor pool, reeking of disinfectant, below the central building. Square, bow-legged young men in skull-caps thrashed the water; their chests were heavy and their skins white. Trainers shouted at them and, occasionally, at me. I found I had no energy, and attributed this to lack of food: not only was there rationing; I had little money.

Occasionally I visited the new wife of my Uncle Humfrey, the general: she had been a princess, and had a Russian servant called Evgeniy, who went round the apartment in white coat and striped trousers, testing the cords of the heavy pictures, lest they crashed on something.

One Sunday I went out to St Cloud to see Michelle, the young French girl that had written to me on my leave several years before. I took the Métro, then a bus. It was windy and snowing, the snow blowing in swirls across the streets. The bus conductor was an elderly man with waxed moustaches: *'Oh la jeunesse!'* he would cry, when young men ran for the bus and leaped on when it was moving; then he would blow on his hands and fasten the chain across the gap at the back of the rear platform. Michelle received me coldly, I thought. Her family was comfortable and middle-class, and lived in an over-decorated house that suited them. The curtains were heavy and tasselled. We had an excellent, rich, Sunday lunch. Michelle's father was a heavy, bald, self-indulgent man with a gold watch and black hairs thick on his large wrists. I had just had my hair cut very short, so that my ears stuck out; my suit was too small for me. After coffee and liqueurs I left in the swirling snow, and never saw Michelle again.

There was a tall boy of seventeen, with curly, reddish-brown hair and enormous enthusiasm, living in the Maison Franco-Britannique. His name was Charles Adeane. He was a great giggler. One evening he and I went to a terrible dance in the central building. Over lemonade during an interval we ran into a cadaverous painter from Chorlton-cum-Hardy, who looked a bit like D. H. Lawrence. This was Frank, who, like Charles, was to become a lifelong friend. He had just returned to Paris after a visit to Manchester. He made a speech about it.

'I saw L. S. Lowry, the painter, in Manchester,' he said. 'I followed him about. He was wearing two overcoats above a long mac. What a man. I had a lovely time, though Manchester is a city of business. I lived in my own dream world. I liked walking round the strangely quiet roads; all was so grey; and the buildings were a funny crimson sooty colour that made you want to touch them; but you couldn't, because they were so far away. The tower of the prison loomed up out of a grey sky which seemed to hug the whole city.

'After Paris it was dead, but it held me in an iron grip on wet, dark, slimy nights: the pavements and cobblestones wet and shiny, and pretty girls going in and out of Marks & Spencer. I wore a mac as black and gleaming as the roads. A dark, wet night found me looking in a shop window full of furniture: cheap, vulgar settees and divans, bedroom suites, chromium-plated ashtrays, model Alsatian dogs, and junk. Well, among all this I saw myself reflected in the mirror of a flashy dressing table: I caught the slime of my mac, then I saw my back reflected in another mirror, which was reflected back again, and I saw my profile. I began to like this, especially as I had a deep red scarf to contrast with the shiny black material. Mind you, the shop was not illuminated, all that being *interdit*; but nearby was a dreary, dim lamp which gave a bit of light and which suited my taste better than a full-dress performance with limelight. I could not tear myself away from admiring my profile, with its beret, the neat collar of the mac, the red scarf, the oily tramlines behind, and those adorable oily cobbles on which many an iron-rimmed wheel of a cart drawn by horses had made an unforgettable din. Well, when I had had enough of admiring myself amid all this junk, I decided to clear off to the end of the road to look at the *Evening News* office, a vast, glass-and-steel construction bathed in a sort of white, phosphorescent mist. I then went into a pub that contained a gathering of poor working-class toughs. They simply couldn't make me out, and I hadn't the courage to stay there very long. But I had a longing to be one of them.'

Frank, a pupil of Léger, lived in a small triangular room without a window just off the Boulevard St Michel; the rest of the house was full of Indo-Chinese cooking ducks on small stoves. Frank was an ardent pianist as well as a painter, and practised for hours in the dark on a silent keyboard. He lived carefully on money left him by his grandfather. His remaining relatives in Manchester and the solicitor that administered his grandfather's estate disapproved of his life in Paris. 'Worthless,' they called it. I knew little about Frank's past, except that he had once got his grandmother's Daimler caught by the tide at Lytham St Anne's in company with a chauffeur called Fred, who had very blue eyes. Frank lived so carefully that when his mistress, in a rage, cut up a Camembert cheese of his with scissors, he left her for ever.

One of Frank's gambits was to take out girls in the rain to Fontainebleau, where he would make them stand in shiny black macs beneath the dripping beech trees. Although he looked no athlete, Frank one afternoon leaped three tables standing together outside the Café de Flore in St Germain-des-Prés; then he went down on his knees, put his shoes on his kneecaps, and crossed the Boulevard St Germain in this fashion, like a dwarf, his mac trailing.

In the Cité Universitaire, between bathing and drinking watered cocoa, I was reading about the life of Flaubert: it had a bad effect on me; like Flaubert, I began to take almost a week to write a paragraph, and would hurl myself, exhausted, on to my bed between each word. Living in the Cité Universitaire was a little like living in the YMCA in Surbiton: so I took a room in the Hôtel Stella, 41 rue Monsieur-le-Prince, in the Latin Quarter. The room, on the top floor, was small, and the floor sloped. There was a view of steep roofs and fantastic chimney pots. Below was a small courtyard at the back of a restaurant: chefs in white hats appeared from steaming doorways and moved about. It was the rule to throw things you did not want out of the window, which annoyed the chefs.

The concierge was helpful. I used to knock on her glass-panelled door, and she would beckon me in to her room of keys and bundles of washing, where we would compare our troubles. Now and again I gave her a tin of coffee, then rare in France: in return she darned my socks and sewed on buttons. One day when my corduroys, furrowed like a ploughed field, were in for repair, she waved to me with a particular flourish and look of pride. I found that she had sewn on the brace-buttons with copper wire. At the same time she made me a gift of some French Army braces, without 'give', but tenacious, which had belonged to her eldest son.

She had sewed on four buttons in this revolutionary fashion, instead of the more normal six. My corduroys, she told me, were always without creases; they would not assume creases even were I to soap the linings of the legs and sleep on them. But she believed they might become more respectable if I had one brace-button, instead of the more normal two, above each other crease at the front – or above where the creases should have been. She was sure that in this way they would hang better.

I cannot pretend that from then on my corduroys were perfect. For one thing they were far too broad and far from malleable, so that when I walked, each leg brushed against the other with a mournful sighing note: after a mile or two friction developed and they became quite hot.

I inscribed at the Sorbonne at last, and sometimes attended lectures. One of my fellow-students was a large Negro from Chicago on a GI grant. 'Man,' he'd say before a lecture, 'this guy'll put you right to sleep.'

I had lunch in student restaurants for the equivalent of nine-pence. It was usually thick green soup and *boudin*, which was black pudding. Each night I cooked myself an egg and ate a slice of a strange slimy cake, very filling and very cheap. When it was really cold, and the authorities were afraid of students' dying off, they used to dole us out free 'Smarties' from an office near the Panthéon. You had to produce your student's card, and then a nurse and an old man in a beret doled out the 'Smarties' with a ladle.

In a students' restaurant I met a student with a game leg who must have been at least forty. His main worry seemed to be about Churchill, and he used to insist on walking up and down the Boulevard St Michel late at night discussing him. 'But is Churchill really a gentleman?' he would ask.

I was noting down the Parisian scene in my notebooks: millions of words accumulated. I noted the increase of hearses in January and the colour of umbrellas in the Luxembourg Gardens. It was useless. Because I was eating so little I often failed to get up in the morning. But several afternoons a week I went and gave English lessons to a French journalist who lived in the Boulevard Raspail. He was trying to make a break-through in the puppet theatre, and a small puppeteer with shiny black hair was usually there saying '*Évidemment, évidemment.*' The journalist, whose name was Paul, had been a POW during the war. He and his wife, Marthe, took me to Tours one week-end to stay with Marthe's mother and stepfather. These people lived in a small house with plush curtains and gilt ornaments, and drank sweet white wine. On their piano was a photograph of de Gaulle. 'Laval was up on that piano not long ago,' Paul told me. 'And poor old Pétain.' We went out in an ancient upright Renault to see the châteaux of the Loire. The car had a small vase of plastic flowers stuck on the windscreen.

An English girl, a dancer, came to stay in Paris. She was big, dark, and strong, and had a nose like a scimitar. She walked with that wonderful, turned-out dancer's walk. We visited a friend of hers, a blonde Russian dancer called Irina. Irina's White Russian father was an old scientist who looked like Trotsky and grew plants in the bath. Irina danced at the Bal Tabarin. Her lover was a small ex-dancer who ran a night-club. One day the English girl and I went up the Eiffel Tower. It was a wonderful, sad, grey day. On the very top there was a fair wind. I took out a grey handkerchief I had bought in Port Said for tuppence; it was made of fake silk and had a hole in it. I let it flutter in the wind, and then let it go. It sailed away, losing height slowly. We watched it till it was almost out of sight above the Champ de Mars, not far from the École Militaire. We went down in the lift, and walked nearly a mile to retrieve the handkerchief from a flower-bed. Then we had a drink in a small bar, clunking our glasses on the zinc-topped counter and shuffling our feet in the sawdust. The Eiffel Tower was visible through a window. That night we saw Irina dance at the Bal Tabarin, drank a good deal, danced ourselves, and came home late. As we walked she put her hand on my shoulder. 'You can't bear being touched, can you?' she said. I saw her to her hotel, and then went down the street to mine: when I reached it I found that I was locked out. I returned to the girl's hotel, told her what had happened, and asked if I could sleep in her room. 'I've got the curse,' she said. She gave a laugh. 'And anyhow,' she said, rather miserably, 'I've never slept with anyone.' 'Nor have I,' I said, and my voice was more miserable than hers. I slept on the floor of her room.

Frank and I decided we would visit Italy. Philippe Siou, a very thin Frenchman, said he would like to come.

Neither Frank nor I were the sort of people that are good at cheap travel. We carried suitcases, both fairly battered, and made of a material that is not exactly cardboard and by no means leather. He wore a beret and a nice, striped blue suit, the coat of which he kept neatly done up on all three buttons, despite the heat. I wore my demobilization suède shoes and a mustard ferreting coat. I describe what he wore to show that we did look all right.

Even so, lifts were difficult to get. At the beginning, in a tram in Turin, we met an old man who had been a coalminer near Chicago and had come back to Italy to die: 'Boys,' he said, 'you can't bum a ride here.'

It may have been that Philippe, the Frenchman, let us down: perhaps, because he was French and had got three Croix de Guerre with the Quatrième Spahis, he did not look at all inexpert: he had no qualms about rucksacks and he wore shorts, above legs that were a great deal more effective than they looked. His rucksack was enormous, full of equipment, and heavy; he handled it as though it scarcely existed.

We went down through Italy pretty slowly. Some days we just lay down with our backs against piles of gravel on the side of the road and did not try to get on. I think our diet, which was mainly bread and plums, may have had something to do with it. We spent one night in the sports stadium in Florence: it was not bad. Frank carried a little methylated spirits stove, and in a village south of Lake Trasimene he made a cup of tea for an old man who had never tasted tea before. The old man was very interested, and told us he had been a blacksmith's assistant. In this village, which was remote, they introduced us to a girl from Manchester who was living above the chemist's. This pleased Frank. Near Siena there was a fearful thunderstorm and we sheltered in a cart standing in a lean-to. In the middle of the storm Frank slid from the cart and fell among a sow and her young and was bitten. There was a ruined castle on the hill opposite, silhouetted against a sky of lightning; and there was strange laughter.

We rode from Arezzo (where Frank had taken us to see the frescoes of Piero della Francesca) to Perugia with an old Alsatian dog in the back of a truck full of wheels of Parmesan cheese. It was hot. When the truck first stopped to pick us up, the driver insisted we climb into his cab; but since there were already three people in the cab, it became crowded. The driver was jolly, and kept hooting his horn at girls and swerving at them. He had a long scar across his forehead which he said had been made by an Abyssinian sabre. He realized how full his cab was when he tore my trousers changing gear; it was then he suggested we climb in the back with the cheeses and the old dog.

That evening we went from Perugia to Assisi, where Peter was buried in the British military cemetery below the town. We called on a fair-haired Englishman, a former sergeant, who kept the cemetery. He was a good man, from the Home Counties, married to an Italian girl. They said they would put us up that night, and told us how to find the cemetery. We washed; and then Philippe and I went down there. It was a fine evening. The cemetery was impeccable. Each grave had a small white wooden cross; the permanent headstones were not yet in place; I preferred the wood. The neat white crosses were so many; a forest of white crosses. It is hard to imagine a hundred, a thousand, a million dead. How many dead can a nation stand?

We searched for Peter's name on the white crosses. Suddenly Philippe, just ahead, called me. He had found the grave and, upon the white cross, the name: Lieut. P. M. Gale, 2nd Bn, Coldstream Guards. Philippe stood there, serious, the thin Frenchman. It was strange to find that name upon the white cross. We looked at it. Then we walked back to the house of the English cemetery-keeper, the former sergeant, and his Italian wife. We ate with them, and slept well that night. The next morning, before we left, I got up early, and went out in the fields towards the cemetery. There was a single dead tree trunk standing in a hedge; dead white. Up on the hill I could see the buildings and walls of Assisi, grey in the early morning.

We slept three in a bed in Rome, in a tired hotel that was full of footsteps. The next day Philippe and I called on some people who were, I suppose, cousins of mine by marriage. I had never met them before. They lived in a palazzo, which was more formidable than we had supposed: at the door was a *carabiniero*, since half the building was occupied by a South American legation. We entered feeling a bit underdressed, Philippe in shorts, I in the ferreting coat. When the footman disappeared to announce us, Philippe – oppressed by the strict budgeting of the past three weeks – wandered round the hall muttering at the walls, which were heavy with Poussins and Fragonards. We had tea with the cousins and an English nanny who had been with the family since 1910. And we were invited to a party to be held that evening.

We hurried back to our hotel, where we attempted to shape up our clothes: I dampened the creases in my trousers, which I hung upside down, the turn-ups pinned in a closed drawer, in the hope that some of the wrinkles would hang out. Philippe worked on his shorts. Frank had disappeared.

Everyone else was in evening dress when we arrived at the party, and there was a rash of European princes, most of them stateless. The poacher's pocket in my ferreting coat was useful: I was able to slip into it handfuls from the buffet. We danced on a flat roof overlooking the Colosseum, which was floodlit. Everyone was rather pleasant.

After it was over we walked to the station, where we had arranged to meet Frank. The three of us reached Naples at dawn, after several hours in the brake van of what was mainly a goods train; and – although I forget why there was nowhere more suitable – we lay down quite comfortably on a pavement where, with our heads on our suitcases, we slept fitfully until midday, watched by small men with sharp eyes.

In the afternoon we were arrested by Customs men in a quiet bay outside Naples. They thought we looked odd. To my surprise, Frank became terribly indignant and said, 'I'm British, I'm British,' over and over again in Mancunian French until the Customs men understood and were sorry. They disappeared in a rowing-boat, reappearing after about an hour, whereupon they gave us fresh sardines.

The next day, Frank, notoriously ill-equipped, borrowed one of my blankets and left on foot in the direction of Pompeii. Philippe and I bought fourth-class tickets and left that night for Tunis in a thin black steamer. A day out of Naples we called at Palermo, where we ate some rather good ice-cream with a French Tunisian grocer, who had made this trip before and knew his way around. He had dark glasses and a stiff canvas hat and was very proud of North Africa. In the café in which we ate the ice-cream was a tall American woman in white socks who said she had never written books so well as in Malvern.

We reached Tunis after a lot of spaghetti and rough weather. A few hours before we were due to arrive, I was in the fourth-class washroom, cleaning my nails with a matchstick, when a small middle-aged Italian came in, accompanied by his son, who asked me if I would be so good as to shave his father. The father then explained that because his own razor was not a safety razor but a 'cut-throat' he was a bit nervous of shaving in so fierce a sea. I did not make a good job of him, and there were a lot of tufts left under his nose, though I tried to hold it out of the way. The little Italian seemed quite pleased. His son watched the operation closely without saying a word.

After a doctor had vaccinated us, Philippe and I went ashore. We took a brown suburban train full of cheerful Arabs and rattled over a stagnant-looking promontory to Carthage, where we slept in a hard bed in a white villa belonging to Philippe's aunt, who was away in Paris. In the morning we sat in a dark café in the Rue de Portugal in Tunis and looked out at the sun through a curtain of metal bottle-tops that clicked in the wind: the large *patron* shouted at a small, laughing Arab boy, who scattered sawdust on the floor and served us coffee. We took to sleeping on the beach at Carthage, since Philippe's aunt's housekeeper was not sure about us. We ate dough-rings which Arab vendors fried in tins of fat above braziers. At last Philippe bought a loaf and took a train. He wrote to me later from the Moroccan desert.

I went on living on the beach until a large Italian family who kept a run-down café let me sleep in their porch and fed me on snails. A strangely-fair-haired boy, aged five, insisted on washing my clothes in the sea, while his grandfather dozed under a eucalyptus tree and talked about his experiences on a Greek island.

Eventually a Frenchman lent me money to buy the cheapest ticket back the way I had come, since a shipping strike prevented return by Marseilles. Italian railwaymen were on strike by the time I reached Rome, because someone had taken a shot at Togliatti, the Communist leader. I reached Paris at dawn five days later with a half-empty tin of bitter marmalade. Madame Marteau, the owner of my *pension*, stuck her head out of the window in a nightcap, protested at the hour, and lowered the front-door key on a string.

I packed up my things, paid for my room for the last time and returned, none the wiser to England. When I got home, Jack Weeks, the gardener, met me: 'Christ, *John!*' he said, swinging a bucket of coal. 'You look awful.'

I have a congenital heart murmur: what this sounds like to a doctor with a stethoscope I have no idea: I imagine it is a mild hooting or whistling. All my life school doctors and Army medical officers, who knew little about hearts, said, when they heard it, 'Can you run? Can you swim?' This irritated me. Yet there have been times when I have wondered if there really was something wrong with my heart. Pure neurosis. Not long after I returned from Paris, I went out to supper and had a lot of gin. Then I ran in the rain more than a mile for a bus. As I lay in bed that night my heart began to flutter: fibrillation, I believe it is called; I was terrified. It went on and on. I got up in the early hours and went to my father's room: 'I'm done for,' I told him. Next day a doctor, not a heart man, came, and said he thought I had had some sort of mild heart attack. Next I saw a heart specialist, who examined me thoroughly, and then laughed. 'You're as fit as a fiddle,' he said.

The heart specialist's daughter was Jill, the ballet dancer, who had black hair and large eyes in a small face with a strong chin and a chipped, upturned nose.

Soon afterwards, Jill's mother and father asked my mother and father and me out to dinner. Jill was there, and wore a black silk dress shot with copper, green and scarlet that had belonged to her grandmother. She was quiet. Her black hair was long, and her face serious. A week or two later I asked her out to dinner in London. We ate in Soho.

Afterwards we walked on damp November pavements to Chelsea, where she shared a flat. Then we walked out on to the Albert Bridge, and looked at the Thames, gleaming, and smelling of oil and mud. That night I could not sleep.

I had to get a job. Journalism seemed the only answer. But there was rationing of newsprint then, and it was hard to get on to a paper. Aunts and friends were helpful. At last I got a job with a group of newspapers in the Midlands. The evening paper was the most important in the group: it was in a square yellow building that smelled of charred sacking. The building was always being enlarged: plaster-board cubby-holes sprouted constantly to house men who had grown too important to live in crowded rooms. My first week, a reporter – with a face burnt when his bomber caught fire in the war – showed me round. Each morning we did the calls: on the police, the fire station and the hospital. We covered inquests and the local magistrates' court. On my first day in court a tramp was prosecuted for burning down a warehouse. 'I thought I'd give them something to remember me by,' he said.

After about ten days I became a general reporter. My shorthand was not immaculate, and caused me pain. Once they discovered that in one of my court stories I had got a magistrate on probation instead of the offender: Ron, the tea-boy, was sent rushing down to the machine-room to stop the first edition which was already thumping out below: 'Hold everything,' he cried, 'Dobby wants a bash.' 'Bashing' was when Mr Whitby, the chief machine-operator, stopped the engines, took a chisel, and slashed the inaccuracy from the rounded metal cast that had the print upon its face. Some papers call this 'blurring': our paper was quite often fairly blurred.

'Dobby' was the editor, Mr Dobson. He had great loose features upon a blue face and a little lawn of ginger hair at the back of his shining skull. He wore green suits and thick oiled shoes that had a strong smell. 'Dobby' was 'carried' by Mr Fedderton ('Feathers'), who really was a journalist. Everything about Fedderton was grey: his hat, his ravaged pike's face, his loose, threadbare suits, engrained with cigarette ash. They said he'd been 'burnt up in Fleet Street' years before, and hinted at a past eaten by grief and disease.

'Nicely now, Gale,' Fedderton would say to me, 'but this is clear as mud: how can a mountain' (it was, I think, a gorse-covered hill that had caught fire) – 'how can a mountain "give trouble"?' Then he would burst into a terrible fit of coughing and throw my story into the waste-paper basket. 'There's a little man below who doesn't like this sort of writing,' he would say, and he would grimace horribly and point downwards through the floor to the office of the proprietor, a small bluebottle in huge horn-rimmed spectacles, who had once sold newspapers on a street corner and now owned racehorses.

On Saturday afternoons the reporters took copy on the telephone: football reports from all the local games, telephoned in by correspondents. This strained my shorthand: 'Barrett flicked the leather to Graves, who shot. Custodian Craddick punched clear of the uprights.' All these reports went into the 'Pink 'un', the Saturday evening football special.

Often at this time I felt ill and depressed: I lived in a mauve world; I felt as though there was something wrong with my insides. At last I mentioned this to my mother, who fixed an appointment for me with a doctor in London she then thought highly of. He came originally from Hungary.

'You've got a limp?' he asked, when I entered his consulting room. 'No,' I said. I tended to limp in those days when I felt self-conscious. He examined me swiftly and thoroughly, obviously thinking little of my symptoms. Then he asked: 'Have you ever slept with a girl, for instance?' 'No, not really,' I admitted. 'Why?' he asked. 'It's easy enough.' He stroked his chin.

'Look,' he said. 'I'd like you to take a small test. Would you mind?' He produced what was, I think, a card, with a lot of shapes and ink-blobs on it: it was a Rorschach test. Upon the doctor's asking me, I told him what the various shapes reminded me of. One, I said, reminded me rather of a rabbit with its guts hanging out. 'Hmm,' he said. I was to call on him next day, when he had analysed his data. Before seeing him, I had had no idea he was a psychiatrist or analyst; I had thought he was a straight physician.

When I saw him next day he said, 'Well, you know, you're tied up in knots. You really are. That's my view. In that test, normal, healthy people should discern human beings in the ink shapes. You made out only things, objects, and unhealthy ones at that – a rabbit with its entrails torn out. There's something missing with you on the human side, in your human relationships. I seriously advise you to undergo psychoanalysis with me: it's a big undertaking; it would mean your giving up your present job in the Midlands and living in London, so that you could come to me every day. I can assure you we don't give these sort of opinions lightly. But you're all in knots.'

'I'll sort myself out,' I said.

'Just you try,' he replied. 'Just you try. Anyhow, I'd think it over.'

I returned to the Midlands, thought it over, and then wrote to the doctor saying I had decided against analysis.

For a time at the paper they put me on a teleprinter on which I tapped messages like 'OK TKS' (OK THANKS) and 'NOW IS THE TIME FOR ALL GOOD MEN TO COME TO THE AID OF THE PARTY' to a fat girl in a red corduroy skirt who worked on the other end.

I took a short holiday in the South of France, where I met some Englishwomen in a pine wood. They used to swig wine sitting on the rocks with nothing on, and were mad on the local plumber, who was small, elderly, unshaven, and as good a drinker as they were. One night they locked me in a room with a war-widow who had blue sheets. 'What's the matter?' she would ask me. 'Did you have too many girls in Paris?' She had small, spidery veins on the inside of her thighs. I remember her standing naked at the window looking out at the sunny morning: then she touched her breasts: 'I think they're still a good shape, don't you? People always say so.' I was twenty-three.

On my return to work, I became a reporter, the only one, on a weekly paper in the group: it was the local paper of a small red-brick spa with large mock-Tudor hotels full of rich, arthritic guests who were taking the waters. My main job was to call on the hotels and find out who the guests were. I also took the names of people at funerals: it was surprising how haughty mourners could be. The mayor of the spa was the manager of the cinema: he was a friend of 'Feathers', whose secondary job was to edit this weekly paper. I used to call on the mayor in his office in the cinema, and he would dictate to me long stories about himself, which 'Feathers' printed at length. After about six months of this, my pay went up from thirty shillings to two pounds a week.

I had digs with a little woman called Mrs Griffiths, who lived with her granddaughter, Topsy. She looked after me well: for supper, kippers and tea; or tripe and mashed potatoes. A school mistress, who used to be visited by a very old 'gentleman friend', had lodgings in the pink house next door to Mrs Griffiths: 'She's no lady,' Mrs Griffiths said.

Some week-ends I would go to see the doctor's daughter, Jill, who was touring Britain with a company. We walked on the grey beach at Skegness: the sky was huge and grey and the sea breathed far off over cold sand; we left Skegness by a flat, wet road past a small gasometer. I saw Jill in Liverpool, and we stayed, rather rashly, in The Stork Hotel: we took a cold ferry, and walked in the mist at New Brighton, to the mournful lowing of foghorns. I saw her in Glasgow: we took the bus to Aberfoyle, and walked in the rusty hills in pouring rain that soaked us to the skin; then we had hot baths and drank whisky in front of a blazing wood fire.

Suddenly I felt I could stay in the Midlands no longer, so I resigned.

At home, my brother Adrian and I spent a week-end pulling ivy and creepers off the house with a rope and a small, upright motor-car belonging to my mother. It had a jumpy clutch. We had torn away most of the ivy from the brickwork and were gathering ourselves for a struggle with the last creeper, while waiting for the little car to cool down.

At this moment Adrian noticed an old washing-up glove lying on the gravel. Without reason – he has never been able to explain it – he picked it up, shook it, and walked over to the yard tap, to which he fastened the glove with string. Then he spun the tap full on, and the glove swelled grotesquely. The water pressure in this area, just below the North Downs, was tremendous. The glove, pink and rubbery, grew and grew, like some new form of life; and as it grew, it groaned and pinged.

We watched, hypnotized and slightly apprehensive. Jack Weeks, the gardener, who had been doing something in the kitchen garden, came through the gap in the tall hedge – I remember he was wearing a belt as well as braces – and stood, shifting his feet and letting out nervous laughs. 'Cor,' he said. This broke the tension. Adrian, who was, I noticed, sweating, stepped forward and turned off the tap.

My grandfather, who had come over for tea from Kent, joined us at this moment, exclaiming, 'Well I never.' He tapped the unearthly shape that had been a glove with his stick, and the glove, held off the ground by its huge, waterfilled fingers, shivered.

This was only the beginning of the business. Adrian, who was on leave and, up to this time, rather bored, became thoroughly preoccupied. He went to the local garage and brought back old inner tubes. These he treated in the same way as the glove; the results were even more remarkable. I remember one inner tube in particular: it had belonged to a tractor and had 'Heavy Duty' stamped on it. It was grey, and it seemed to be able to stand anything. Adrian experimented with it for about a week.

He fastened it to the tap, and it grew and grew until it resembled a great blind whale. I don't know how many gallons he got into it, but it must have been something like a thousand. Sometimes he would climb up on to it and smoke a cigarette. Cars passing our front gate would draw up to watch. I felt that if anything gave way there might be some sort of damp combustion. I kept to the house a good deal.

One evening I was reading, glancing from time to time towards the yard, when there was a noise like agonized elastic: I caught sight of Adrian, on his back, being carried along in a surge of water. I leant out of the window: for a moment the air seemed filled with a thin, lifeless crying which faded away over the trees. Adrian came in looking a bit white, and very wet. He never tried any more experiments. It was a curious business.

I wanted to become a writer. But this seemed impossible at home with my family. I went to live on a farm in Hampshire, where I laboured away to turn out mechanical stories with artificial plots. The farmer's daughter was a dancer, a fine, big girl who came home at week-ends and swung a silken leg; but my thoughts were elsewhere. The farmer's capable, hard-working wife had a large, retarded man, known as 'Basher', in her charge. A bad-tempered rook also lived in the house: it was the terror of the cats, except in the spring, when it would fall in love with one of the eunuch tabbies, and build the tabby a nest on the hotplate of the kitchen stove: then, by judicious pecking, it would direct the cat to this nest and force it to remain there sitting on imaginary eggs.

The farmer claimed he could regulate the sex of animals and men by the state of the moon at the moment of conception: he said he had never failed with his cows and sheep; nor with his own family. My parents had tried this formula, and had produced nothing but boys.

I went down with jaundice so severe that I turned from yellow, to orange, to blue, to purple. I left the farm and returned home. Recovered, I got a job on the 'Crossbencher' column of the *Sunday Express*.

That summer my parents divorced. A day or two later Jill, the ballet dancer, and I walked in Hyde Park on a fine evening. 'Look,' she said. 'Haven't we known each other long enough? You've got a job now. Either we get married, or I'm off.' I said we'd better get married. We bought a Georgian engagement ring with three small diamonds from the late Moshe Oved, at Cameo Corner, near the British Museum. If he liked a person Mr Oved would sell her something for very little; or he would even lend her a piece of jewellery, saying: 'It likes you.'

The day before our wedding a man rang up and asked me to have a drink at the Café Royal. He was a writer, a former journalist, who had once given me advice about entering journalism. I knew that he worked for MI5. He was an intelligent man, round and dark, and wore glasses with heavy black frames. He filled me up with pink gin, then he said, 'Look. I think you know some of the work I'm doing. Would you like to help us? We've looked up your Army career, and so on, and think you'd be rather suitable. At the moment we're rather anxious to find out where Peter — is, and what he's up to. Would you keep your ears to the ground? Anyway, think it over. Later, after you've worked for us a bit, you'll probably get paid something, and be given bigger jobs. Going up to the docks at Liverpool, and so on.' I was full of gin he'd paid for, and did not like to refuse. Instead I said: 'I'm getting married tomorrow.' 'Good heavens,' he said. 'I'm sorry. I didn't know.'

I went round to pick up my father. We were to drive down to Blechingley, and spend the night at the Manor House before the wedding next day. My father told me he'd just got married again: 'We thought we'd beat you to it,' he said. I told him how I had been asked to work for MI5. 'Don't touch it with a barge-pole,' he said. 'That's what I think. As you know, I was in something like that during the war. They can be awful asses. Do you want to get tied up in that sort of thing in peacetime? Do you believe in it? Your job's to be a journalist, isn't it?'

I felt the same. I didn't think I'd be any good at spying on other people: I couldn't keep secrets and disliked them. I had an impractical idea that if a country had no secrets and told the truth there would be less to fear; people loved secrets because it made them feel important. Spying and tailing were scarcely my line: no doubt I had a streak of the *voyeur* in me; but not for this. That night I wrote a letter to the round, dark man with the heavy black-framed glasses, explaining why I couldn't work for MI5.

Jill and I were married in church. I had said, without any great feeling, that I would have preferred a registry office, since we were both agnostics. My brother Adrian drove me to the church in his old open Morris. I felt like jumping out. Jill was twenty-one; I was just twenty-five. I had felt we would marry, ever since I had seen her sunbathing as a thirteen-year-old girl one day during the war.

We could only take one week-end off after the wedding. We drove to a rather smart pub in the New Forest. The next day we visited Tyneham and Warbarrow, which I had not seen since 1939. Tyneham had been dead seven years, stripped of human life as though by plague. The grey cottages, built of local stone, stared with sightless eyes, their windows gone or patched with black squares of tarred felt. The wind lived in Tyneham, slamming doors with a ghostly hand, heedless of the scores of rabbits that rippled the nettles thick about the buildings.

The old church was ringed with barbed wire and its path hidden by grass. But the small graveyard, watched over by the pale stump of a great elm, was still neat; and the tombstones, the oldest of them scoured thin by time and the salt air from the sea, were strangely white.

During the war the Army commandeered Tyneham and six thousand acres about it, including Warbarrow Bay, turning it into a battle-training ground for tanks. When Jill and I visited it, the day after we were married, it was open to the public while the staff of the gunnery school was on leave. The inhabitants, compulsorily evacuated in 1943, would probably never return.

So Tyneham remained, blind and lonely. Tyneham House, built in 1583, of the same grey stone, stood deserted among noble trees: as we walked round it a tawny owl, disturbed by our voices, slipped from the eaves. The garden of the house had run wild amid barbed wire, and the windows were blindfolded with sheets of black corrugated iron; a small pond on what was once a lawn was stagnant, choked with weed beneath which huge water beetles were gliding; the skull of a stag's head, pierced by the rusty screw that once secured it to panelling, lay among rotting leaves beside the drive; bees, which had made their home in an outhouse, murmured in an avenue of limes.

As we walked down to Warbarrow Bay, a fox, knowing little of the ways of humans, ran past us as carelessly as a dog.

There was something elemental about Warbarrow then. Although Jack Miller's cottage would have needed little to make it habitable, this did not feel a place of man or even of animals. The cottage on the beach, on a mound of stones to protect it from the gales of winter, might have grown by itself. A boathouse near by had been blasted by a mine and its metal roof torn and crumpled into some primeval shape: a cow's skeleton lay on the sand; in the small valley behind the bay, stunted trees, hanging their heads to the east to escape the wind off the sea, seemed prehistoric. We climbed the rocky knob of the Tout: the tell-tale bald patches, made by footsteps on the earth, had gone, being covered with coarse sea-grass; but I could still tell by certain distinctive stones how near we were to the top. At the summit, embedded in rock, was the large metal ring that had secured a cannon in the Napoleonic wars. The wind was fresh, but there was not a single gull upon it. The blue hull of Portland Bill lay fifteen miles away across the water to the west. Gad Cliff, with the brown and rust-coloured overhang, rose high to the east. Beyond Gad we could see inland behind Tyneham to the woods and old smooth hills of a silvery green. The only moving thing in sight at Warbarrow this day was a lone cormorant, circling high some way inland as though even the sea was empty of fish.

Jill and I had a week's honeymoon later: In Paris we called on Frank, who was still living in his small triangular room without a window just off the Boulevard St Michel. We pretended to be Indo-Chinese. We climbed silently to the fourth floor, and called his name in what we hoped were Chinese voices. Frank, sitting in the dark at his silent keyboard, got to his feet, and opened the door. We pulled him out, blinking, into the street; then we took him, looking crumpled and sawdusty, to Rumpelmayer's in the rue du Faubourg St Honoré, where he told Jill, whom he had never met before, that his ambition was to have a bath with a conger eel.

The *Sunday Express* sacked me almost as soon as I returned to work. It was the time of the newsprint shortage, and several others lost their jobs with me. I got a job with a news agency. 'Why are you trying to be a journalist?' asked the large Scots editor who interviewed me. The agency was a factory, and the atmosphere close, noisy and mechanical, against the whine of backstairs politics.

Jill had a job in a night-club in Piccadilly, which had then just opened. The owner was a Hungarian, a small, elderly man with a moustache, gold watch, hump back, and a certain courtesy. His wife was large and silver-haired. I enjoyed watching rehearsals. A plump redhead called Josée rehearsed the dancers. She would tap her foot and say: 'Yada, dada, pom-pom, yada yada, pom-pom, yada pom-pom-pom-pom. Ye gaads.' Then she would demonstrate to the girls how to walk like a tart.

Waiters watched and occasionally whistled softly.

The opening night came, with tinsel and bad food. Orson Welles, a huge, brooding figure, sat in the shadows with a cigar, waiting for a blonde showgirl called Jane. The girl dancers, including Jill, complained about the corned beef sandwiches they were given for supper between acts.

The news agency continued to be unbearable: one morning I resigned. I decided to write at home in our flat in a large decaying house north of Notting Hill. Jill was making enough money in the night-club to keep our heads above water. I was writing painfully one night when Jill rang me up from the night-club; she was laughing: a man had sent her a note backstage, and was now buying her champagne; she had just discovered he had been a fellow-officer of mine in the Coldstream. 'Come round,' she said. 'He's a bit embarrassed.'

Two days later Jill said: 'D'you know something? I think I'm having a baby.' We tried to work out when we had achieved this; it was, we decided, under a holly tree in the New Forest, not far from the Rufus Stone, on the same fine Sunday-evening that a publican had tried to sell us a truckload of monkey-dung.

Jill said she would go on dancing. I went on writing; but I was apprehensive about money. I kept notebooks:

Names: Hotcrutch Fifoot; Crumber Broskit; Sebag Lucas; Mountain Lawless.

Young man picks up tart: they kiss: her pale lips stretch and stretch and stretch until they engulf his head and suffocate him.

At night we hear distraught owners calling their dogs: one is a giant, middle-aged blonde who has a black chow with a purple tongue. By day a postman opposite cleans a tricycle: he wears bedroom slippers and has a green plastic bowl of hot water.

One sunny afternoon I was looking out of the window at the cross roads at the end of our street: I could see two cars approaching the cross roads from different directions, and sensed they were going to collide: they did.

Once I saw a group of Indians staring upwards, hypnotized by a windmill.

I like to see lighted trains passing at night. And it is good to look out of the window of the flat under the stars and hear the dogs woofing in the distance.

There are men who take as wives or mistresses women that they feel will glitter and do them honour in public; these women, stripped of clothes and pretence, may not really please them. I prefer a quiet woman, who is beautiful naked, for me, rather than beautiful in clothes, for others. I often think I will write about Jill's body: why should I not, if painters paint their wives?

Sometimes in the morning I watched Jill as she slept after coming back late from the night-club: though so dark, she had a single fair hair on her cheek, which might almost have grown from me to her: it reminded me of the hybrid tree, half-yew half-holly, that I had found in the garden of the Manor House when a boy.

A middle-aged Jewess in the rag trade lived in the flat below us. She had a red Austin convertible with an electrically-operated hood, and you could hear the hood purring up or down when she went out or came back at night. Her lover was a small, curly-haired Jewish all-in-wrestler called Al: they had fights, and screamed and swore, often staggering outside screaming in the rain. She was a kind woman, and scarcely minded when our bath overflowed and the water seeped through the floor, bringing down the ceiling of her bedroom when she and Al were making love.

The acrobatic dancer in the night-club had a little wizened mother who never spoke: while waiting for her daughter after the show she read the Bible. The acrobatic dancer was married; she told Jill she had had five miscarriages. The proprietor of the night-club was trying to make the dancers sit on old men's knees.

At last Jill stopped dancing: she had danced the can-can for four months with a baby inside her. 'Have you a craving?' asked another dancer, the then wife of Edmund Purdom, imagining Jill might long for champagne, smoked salmon or oysters. 'Yes,' Jill replied, with crumbs on her lips and her eyes large and dark in her small face. 'Marmite toast.'

Our char, Nellie Carter, was a huge, dark-haired woman with a bandaged leg. She was determined Jill was going to have trouble with the baby: 'When's your birthday, dear?' she asked Jill. 'February 10, you say Oh, Aquarius, the water-carrier: you'll have swelling legs, dear: you can always tell.'

I wrote on in the small, oppressive flat. Most afternoons a man came down the street pushing a handcart, its wheels crackling on the gravel: 'Haroungh', he would cry; it was a desolate sound, and always brought me to the window: he was a big fellow with a ravaged face, wearing a cap perched high on his ginger hair, a mac, and off-white gym slippers. Empty sacks, neatly folded, hung across the side of his cart. But I never knew the meaning of his cry. Was he wishing to buy or sell? He stopped frequently, bellowed 'haroungh', and stared up defiantly at the windows, hoping to catch an unwary face peering from behind lace curtains; then he would knock the side of his cart with a big ring on his left hand, making a hollow sound. At last he would round the corner at the end of the street and disappear, the cry, 'haroungh', growing fainter on the wind.

The baby was due towards the end of January. We went down to the house of Jill's parents at Blechingley. A middle-aged maternity nurse with ginger hair arrived, but the baby did not. The nurse, Jill in full sail, and I walked slowly through the fields and woods below the North Downs: there was a strange winter sunlight, which shone silver on the plough and the bare trees; it was seasonless weather; I could almost believe it was summer, a summer too cold for leaves to come upon the trees. The nurse and I were scarcely friends; the baby did not come. At last, on a Sunday, I took Jill out in her mother's ancient Baby Austin, and we drove fast up and down a bumpy track: Merlin, the spaniel, was sick in the back; the baby clung on. The following Saturday Jill said she felt something happening at last. It began to snow. Her uncle, a G.P., visited her; he said the baby would not arrive till the next day, and went off to a party. Not long after he had left the baby started coming. Jill's father, the heart specialist, who had not delivered a child for years, came up and nervously dabbed a piece of cotton wool soaked in chloroform in the direction of Jill, in the hope of slowing things down; he looked green. I was beside her and he actually dabbed the chloroform at me, nearly putting me out.

'Oh,' said Jill. 'Oh, he's pushing.'

We couldn't get anyone to answer the telephone at the party that her uncle had gone to. In the end we did get him, and he turned up just in time: he was kind and gentle, and delivered the baby beautifully. It was a black-haired girl with huge eyes.

When Jill got up after having the baby, whom we called Joanna, she said it felt as though the bones were coming out of her feet. Her grandfather, aged ninety-two, visited her, and asked her if she had enough milk. Joanna did not like her nose being touched, and frightened herself with enormous farts. She slept like a grown-up, her chin resting in the palm of her hand. She looked very old. When we returned to the flat in London, she held her breath when we carried her upstairs. It seemed remarkable that anything so small could cope with the fog and soot of London. She got miniature gooseflesh when Jill soaped her with cold hands before her bath. Before her feed she gave agonized gasps of anticipation. Seen through the end of her feeding bottle she looked like a little pig. You could hear the milk landing with thumps in her stomach. Afterwards she had high-pitched hiccups which shook her body. Her sprouting pink toes gripped like a monkey's and expresssed her mood. Her hair had the smell of a kitten's. I could tell from Jill's tread in the next room whether or not she was carrying Joanna in her arms. Sometimes Joanna lay on her front like a small bird, with her hands behind her, the palms upwards. Once her face was soaked with the spray of Jill's milk, and looked surprised. The next night I dreamed that Jill suckled a mangy bulldog pup. I woke with a start, and found her preparing to give Joanna her early-morning feed: I told Jill what I had dreamed, and laughed: as I was laughing, she aimed a squirt of her milk into my open mouth; it tasted unpleasantly sweet.

Because the flat was so small and had neither garden nor balcony, we decided to keep Joanna in a cage outside the window. It was an exaggerated parrot cage, made of what is known as elephant wire. An expert, a small man in a brown hat, came to fix it up. He assembled it in a few easy movements and screwed it on to the window-sill, adding a couple of metal supports for good measure. Next, he sat in it, bent nearly double, and bounced up and down to give us confidence. Then he went away.

Certainly the cage was extraordinarily secure. All the same, I must confess that Jill and I did lean out and peer a bit nervously through its bars at the spiked railings far below. But at last, holding our breath, we picked up the basket containing Joanna, then less than a month old, and thrust her out into space. Simultaneously, a number of startled and elderly female faces appeared from behind lace curtains in the windows opposite.

Although they became familiar with the sight of a caged baby, the faces never altogether lost their look of shocked surprise. And in cold weather there were hostile murmurings among the neighbours, the word 'cruelty' being audible.

Yet, whatever the psychological risks of the cage, Joanna did well enough. She was nicely sunburnt; she became apparently immune to frost, instantly pulling off any glove or woollen boot and dropping it at the feet of the milkman; she watched traffic and shouted at passers-by; she was a fine imitator of dogs and rag-and-bone men and a passionate admirer of the Salvation Army. And she escaped one regular experience of babies in cramped surroundings: she was not trodden on.

When there was snow or an east wind, Jill zipped her up in a sort of sack with armholes, made from a worn-out blanket: even in this she humped about quite actively, abusing people in the street below and getting more opportunity for exercise than could be provided by the largest pram. We gave the cage a routine test-shake every morning, and we were always on the look-out for any indication of height-consciousness on the part of its occupant. But the cage gave us no misgivings, and Joanna remained unperturbed.

At a year old, when watching some particularly stimulating sight – a dog fight, a burst sack of coal, a man cranking a dead motor-car – she developed a tendency to whistle and bang her head on the roof of her prison. Soon she grew out of it altogether. But it gave her an admirable start.

I got a job on the *Observer* and began to learn a bit about England. The majority of the population would never accept me as a *working man*. Odd.

> Seen from a train, a man walking
> By a bridge in the rain:
> Grey half-moon of riveted metal.
> Lonely man, like every man, in the rain;
> And the glistening rails part,
> Come together, part again.
> And the signal is green.

One week there was trouble in the docks, and I was sent down to the East End of London to find out what the dockers were feeling. I went into a pub where the bitter was so sour and watery I felt it must do me good.

'They're dockers,' said a man playing shove-halfpenny, pointing at some darts players.

One of the players broke off his darts and came up. He was tall and pale, with a brown check cap. He gave his view of the strike:

'If you arst me, you won't get anything out of the guvner without disciplinary action. But if you have a good guvner, and he looks after you, then you'll look after him. The twenty-five bob we're after now doesn't make much difference to me. But it's when I get older and can't graft, can't do piecework: what'll happen if I can only bring home eight-pound-odd? I'd have to scarper to get an extra two pound. You've got to keep the home happy; yourself, an' all. When all's said and done, it's the wife and children. The home. They say trucking bacon's the easiest job on the wharf. But you get down and try it; nothing's easy in the docks; you're on your feet all day. It's not easy being a working man. Let me tell *you*.'

'What do you think I am?' I asked. 'I work.'

'You? What do you get?' he asked.

'No, no, easy,' some of his mates said.

'I started on a paper at thirty bob a week,' I said.

'I know. And your old man helped you out.'

'Well. Yes.'

That night I returned to the flat, and found Jill terrified.

'Someone's in the lavatory,' she said. 'The door won't open. Feel it.'

The week before there had been a particularly colourful murder in the neighbourhood, still unsolved. I strode through the bathroom of the flat and gave the lavatory door a tug: it gave a little, then held. There was no doubt about it; somebody was holding the door from the inside. I went into the hall, and picked up a heavy cherry-walking stick, relic of my Army days. I felt it and shook it, gripping the thick wood. Then I remembered the murder the week before. I put down the stick, went to my desk in the next room, opened the bottom drawer, and pulled out a wooden holster: the Mauser parabellum, which I had brought back from Germany at the end of the war, and which had remained locked in my desk ever since. I slid the machine-pistol from its butt and then clicked the butt into position. I put no round in the breech. I walked back into the bathroom, aimed the parabellum at the lavatory door, and shouted: 'Right. Come out. I'm armed.'

The door opened slowly, and out came Frank. Jill burst out laughing: she had known it was him.

The next day, Jill, Frank and I visited my grandfather's farm at Crockham Hill. There was a field full of pigs surrounded by an electric fence. We dangled carrots just in front of the fence, and when the young pigs came for the carrots their noses touched the wire and they received a mild electric shock, and squealed. They soon learnt there was something odd about those carrots.

In May 1953 Jill and I went on holiday to Benidorm, not far from Alicante, in Spain. There was one cheap hotel, the Planesia, upon a rock. On the long deserted beach we met a Swiss priest, who had been sent on holiday by his village: all his life he had dreamed of seeing the Mediterranean.

The owner of the Planesia had a limp and a marvellous voice: he sang to us at meals. A German couple turned up: he was a painter, formerly a pupil of Léger; she was a singer. We had no car, and the Germans took us about in their battered Volkswagen: once they drove us in it up a long flight of steps. The painter wanted to find and paint a gipsy girl dancer, and we visited gipsy encampments. Eventually he decided to paint Jill as a gipsy. She sat solemnly to the German, who in the end turned her into an Arab, with a towel wrapped round her head like a turban.

In Spain we conceived James. The time came for us to leave. After we had paid our bill, the owner of the hotel sang us the 'Ave Maria'.

At last we moved to our small house in the suburb. We wondered if the baby would be born on Jill's birthday, 10 February. Jill's mother came to stay. In the evenings after work, while we waited for the baby, I scraped all the varnish off my desk to reveal the oak. It was a slow, satisfying job. After supper on 11 February, when I had almost finished the desk, Jill said the baby was coming. Her mother and I drove her to a nursing home on Hampstead Heath. My father had said he would give us two armchairs if Jill gave him a grandson.

I finished scraping the varnish off my desk. Then my mother-in-law and I went to bed. It was bitterly cold: she had a bath; the wind whistled through the grating in the outside wall of the bathroom. It was then that she stuffed into the grating a newspaper, with, upside down, the headline: 'WHOSE FOOT IS ON THE BRAKE?' I was to look at it often in the years to come.

In the middle of the night Jill shouted to me, as though in a dream, that we had had a son. I woke up, turned on the light, and saw that it was 3.30 a.m. I considered for a bit; then I got out of bed and went out on to the landing. My mother-in-law at that moment opened the door of her room. We went downstairs and telephoned the nursing home. 'Yes, Mr Gale,' said the sister. 'Mrs Gale had a fine son at 3.30.' I made a pot of tea for my mother-in-law and myself. We could sleep no more than night.

My father gave Jill and me two armchairs: light oak legs, light oak at the end of the arms; brown corded material with a simple red pattern. They are still the best chairs we have.

In September 1956, not long after our youngest daughter, Kiki, was born, the paper sent me to Egypt as their Cairo correspondent. I could not take Jill and the children. I was still painting the outside of our small house in the suburb by torchlight at ten-thirty the night before I left. Anglo-Egyptian relations were strained; but few guessed what was coming.

If you lacked perspective in Cairo or were oppressed by the problems of Egypt, it was best to go up into the old city and climb the minaret of the Mosque of Ahmed Ibn Tulun. You circled the minaret as you climbed, and in the dust on the steps were the legs of chickens and the skeletons of rodents dropped by the kites gliding all day in a metal sky. When you reached the top, you looked out upon a city of nearly three million people: in the clear light the sand-coloured houses of the old city appeared clustered about the young skyscrapers of modern Cairo, which was some way behind. It was not the roar of a great northern city that came up to you, but the sound of many voices, edged by the desolate cries of men with something to sell. It was alive and brazen.

To the north-east was the citadel of Salah El-Din (Saladin) with its deep well, down which Mabrouk the Dragoman liked to bellow '*Allahu akbar*' ('God is Great'); and the high Turkish-looking mosque of Mohammed Ali, with twin minarets like pencils; and, beyond, the great limestone quarries from which the blocks of the Pyramids were hewn. To the south, dark blue and distant in the haze, were the Pyramids themselves.

It was the centre of a world and a place to dream dreams. Did Garmal Abdul Nasser come up here as a boy?

One evening in Cairo I went to a night-club not far from where I was living. It was quite late: the oriental dancers, who had done their act, were joining the customers. I asked one of them to dance with me. She was called Ismat.

'Don't you think I look like Cleopatra?' she asked. 'A German told me I did.'

She fanned herself with what seemed to be an ostrich feather. We drank at the bar: she said she didn't really like whisky, and drank little. She seemed to want to go; at last we did. We climbed into an old Chevrolet taxi (the grey whipcord on the seats reminded me of that in my grandfather's Vauxhall nearly thirty years before): the driver was young, and as we drifted along through the Cairo night, dusty and aromatic, he fiddled with his driving mirror so that he could see my companion reflected in it. We drew up at the house I had been lent. I paid off the taxi, and we went inside. Ismat, wearing an evening dress and a white lace shawl over her shoulders, sat down at the piano and tinkled it with one finger.

'Do you really think I look like Cleopatra?' she asked.

At last we went into the bedroom. The night now felt almost cool. She undressed slowly, looking at herself in the long mirror: her clothes lay in a froth on the floor at her feet. When she turned round she had a tiny square of sticking plaster above the elbow on her right arm: I was a little nervous about this, and asked her what it was; she laughed, and said her Lebanese boy-friend had burnt her with his cigarette when they had had too much to drink. 'You're so cold,' she said angrily afterwards. *'You're so cold.'*

On a Tuesday night, a young Egyptian reporter, discussing the news that had just come through of the Israeli attack in the Sinai Desert, remarked: 'Britain, France, and America must now surely stop this aggression against us. Perhaps it will even help bring about a solution of the Suez Canal dispute.'

At that moment an Englishman on the far side of the room gave a shout. We went over to where he was standing watching the Reuter ticker. Sir Anthony Eden's ultimatum was coming up. People couldn't believe what they read; they said nothing, at first. But few Egyptians were slow in believing that the ultimatum to Egypt and Israel was exploiting the Israeli attack for the basest motive: occupation of the Canal Zone – collusion was mentioned straight away. We went out into the soft night and back to our hotels and houses, feeling that anything was possible.

'What answer could Nasser have given to the British and French ultimatum, except "We resist"?' was the reaction of young Egyptians next day.

The friend who had lent me his house had returned, and I was back in my hotel. That morning an elderly guest was so surprised by the happenings that he came down in the hotel lift wearing only one shoe.

Air-raid warnings in Cairo and bursts of anti-aircraft fire over the city caused no great stir. Sudanese servants bellowed *'Noor'* ('lights') when the sirens sounded. Soon they were shouting *'Noor'* in blacked-out hotel corridors in the heat of the day; it didn't seem quite right for Englishmen, even if interrupted in their reading, to protest at this.

In the middle of one of the first night raids, someone said he had just heard over Cyprus Radio that Mr Selwyn Lloyd, the Foreign Secretary, had told the House of Commons it was 'untrue that Cairo had been bombed'. Since Cairo is very concentrated, and military targets in the suburbs were not far from the centre of the city, Mr Lloyd's denial sounded a little academic.

In the bar of the hotel, lit by a dim blue light, the correspondent of *The Times* softly played his guitar and sang the sad words of 'The Foggy Foggy Dew'.

One relaxation at this time was to see how they were getting on with the burning of secret papers up at the British Embassy. The Embassy staff had been cut to a minimum, and red-faced figures in PT shorts and gym shoes were burning giant mounds of papers. 'The funeral pyre of British integrity,' remarked a spectator.

The British Ambassador, Sir Humphrey Trevelyan, was making his last official calls in an open khaki Buick with the usual Egyptian police guard. The sound of the bombs had been his first intimation of our attack. Normally he rode around in a black-and-yellow Rolls-Royce like a wasp. 'Thank God he's not using the Rolls today,' someone remarked. 'Its colour just about sums up British intentions in the eyes of Egyptians now.'

One afternoon the air-raid hooters sounded and guns opened up: there was a sound of jet aircraft flying low, followed by a mighty crump: two fighter bombers, flying at about eight hundred feet, appeared in a climbing turn, followed by black puffs of anti-aircraft fire. Against the sun, they appeared to be twin-boomed. Shrapnel rained on the flat dusty roofs of small shops below; word went round that the heaviest explosion was a plane crashing half a mile away. Was it an English pilot?

A young Egyptian, roused from his afternoon sleep, appeared in pyjamas on the balcony of the seedy tenement opposite. He smiled and shrugged.

'What are you doing to us?' asked a small Egyptian downstairs in the foyer of the hotel. He was a university professor and had a Scots wife. He had been in London during the blitz. A jet sliced overhead and his small daughter slid down into her chair and put her fingers in her ears. It wasn't easy to answer the small man's question.

At dusk, a Sudanese in white robe and skull-cap came up with me on to the hotel roof high above Cairo. He was a simple man. We looked out over the city in the soft light, over the strange complex of sand-coloured buildings, to the slender minarets of the mosque of Mohammed Ali, and beyond to the bare grey

Moqattam Hills. Pillars of smoke from burning airfields and fuel dumps stained the sky.

The Sudanese spoke a slow Arabic: 'Are you English?' he asked. 'Only four countries are with England. I read it in the paper.'

The next morning, the fourth day of bombing, a large party of foreign correspondents toured bombed areas. We drove deep into the country, through groves of tall palm trees that looked almost prehistoric. There were fields of sweet corn, mud huts, peasant women in black robes, small, padding children, astonished buffalo.

Guns opened up, we pulled into the side of the road. English Venoms, well ahead of anti-aircraft bursts, were dive-bombing. It was an odd feeling.

We visited the wireless masts at Abu Zaabal. Two were down. We were beginning to feel that casualties must be small. But there had been six direct hits on the criminal prison next door: stone buildings were flattened, and bodies lay in the hot sun beside craters filled with scummy water.

A big corporal with a tommy-gun gestured towards our group. 'Are they English?' he asked.

'No, Americans,' our Egyptian guide said quickly.

A heavy German correspondent was in his element, appraising damage caused by British arms. He had been a bomber pilot.

'Five hundred kilos from high altitude,' he said, inspecting the craters with admiration.

An Egyptian major spoke to one of my English colleagues: 'I am sure we have met before.' The major must have known we were not Americans. 'What is the meaning of all this?' he asked. There seemed little to say.

Before we left, the major turned and shook our hands, remarking: 'Well, anyhow, very good luck.'

As we walked away, a small Japanese journalist, who knew us, looked up with a grin: 'Ah,' he said, 'so you are Americans?'

At lunch, plain-clothes police came to our hotel. They told us, politely, that we were to be confined to indoors. On the stairs in the black-out that night a colleague blundered into a bulky figure. 'Damn!' he exclaimed. 'I wish I could get out of this blasted hotel.' 'Ah, but that will be very difficult,' came the amused reply. It was one of the police officers.

Next day the Egyptian Air Force, whose headquarters had been destroyed, commandeered our hotel. We were told to pack. Two wing-commanders, accompanied by detectives, searched us and our rooms. They were apologetic. 'We are very sorry to have to do this. But your Government has done us a great wrong.'

British journalists were taken under escort to the Semiramis Hotel. We were politely but closely guarded – and not allowed to talk to anyone outside our party or to leave the hotel – for the next three weeks.

At one of our first meals in the Semiramis, a senior colleague ordered fish. On its arrival he produced an eye-glass, examined his plate, called the head waiter, and thundered: 'What! No *sauce Hollandaise* at the Semiramis Hotel?' We told him that there was a war on, and that we might need all the friends we could get.

Our only complaint about the luxury of our confinement could have been that we were a bit liverish. We lay staring at the ceiling. I knew by now that British intelligence had planned a counter-revolution with men that had been close to King Farouk.

'Someone I knew in our Embassy asked me to come and see him,' an Englishman had told me. 'I went to his office, which was in half-darkness because our bombing had started. He was sitting behind his desk.

' "We're thinking of mounting a little plot," this man at the Embassy told me.

'He eventually gave me twenty thousand Egyptian pound notes and asked me to deliver them to an important Egyptian who would be at a certain map reference at a certain time. I should have refused, but somehow didn't like to. It was all on the old-boy net. Someone lent me a very old and very small car, and I put the money in the boot and set off. When I got to the map reference I found it was in the middle of an Egyptian Army camp. I turned round, took the money back to the man at the Embassy and told him that someone had got the map reference wrong and that I disliked the whole idea of the plot anyhow. The sign for the start of the counter-revolution was to be the playing of a record of a well-known Egyptian woman singer after the news on Cyprus

Radio, but no one in British intelligence seems to have realized that by this time the Egyptians would be jamming Cyprus Radio.'

Our internment in the Semiramis continued to be comfortable. An Egyptian plain-clothes officer occasionally came in, grinning, to our room to talk. He challenged us to that test of strength in which each man places his right elbow on a table and, with his forearm vertical, clasps his opponent's hand and tries to force it down. The police officer and I could not budge each other's forearm an inch. Now and again we took steam baths, where we were trapped in overheated boxes and then pummelled by a famous Graeco-Roman wrestler, who assured us that everything would be 'aw-l-l right'. Sometimes in the hotel we were accosted by small boys collecting money for wounded Egyptian soldiers. One day we read in an Egyptian newspaper that an orchestra in Worthing had decided on some important occasion not to play 'The Triumphal Entry of the Egyptian Army' from *Aida*.

Once the Egyptian Information Department took us out under armed guard and showed us a film of the effects of the British attack on Port Said. There were shots of the bodies of dead women and children. Afterwards the lights went on, and we sat blinking and feeling none too good. Only our senior colleague felt like speaking: he produced his eye-glass and demanded of an Egyptian official: 'Now look here, when's that doctor coming to see about my dysentery?'

Often during our internment in the hotel we would look out at dusk over the Nile, over the low trees with their broad, dusty leaves, towards the original headquarters of the Revolutionary Council, where Nasser sometimes still worked: a building reminiscent of a small Brighton Pavilion, with the minaret of a mosque rising from the roof. Once it lay directly beneath a pale sliver of moon; often it was silhouetted against an astonishing sunset; a felucca, with a sail like a shark's fin, might pass upstream, struggling against the flood waters of the Nile; the air would be still and soft, and we would be filled, quite suddenly, with a sense of the ripe hopelessness of Egypt, as though no man, however strong, could make anything of her.

I shall not forget the humanity of the Egyptians throughout the Suez affair. A young typist, mother of twins, remarked during the bombing: 'Oh, I'm worried all right. But it's only crackpots in the office who say things against individual Englishmen.' A Cairo vet, seeing us during internment, incommunicado and under guard in the hotel, sent us a round of drinks. He didn't know us, but had once, before the Anglo-French attack, admired the condition of the dog of a fellow-correspondent.

At last, after one false alarm, we were told that we were to be expelled.

In the aircraft from Cairo to Naples, we dozed, lulled by the engines. Most of us were to some extent refugees. At Naples we changed planes for Zurich. As we climbed steeply to avoid bad weather over the Alps, the Swiss stewardess, digging in her heels against the slope, came down the cabin, distributing English newspapers: the first we had seen for a month. An account of a debate in the House of Commons caught the eye, with the faces of 'Suez Group' Conservatives smiling confidently from the page. They were discussing clearance of the Canal and the withdrawal of British troops. It wasn't easy to concentrate, but one paragraph stuck in the mind:

Mr Butler (answering a question): 'No, sir, I think the honour of our country is safely in the keeping of the Government.'

We spent a night in Zurich and reached London next day, a grey Saturday. At the paper I was at first too excited to write, so I talked to a friend, who wrote an impeccable story under my name. Jill, her black hair curling strongly in the damp air, turned up at the office in a green coat with a grey fur collar. She brought me a bottle of whisky, and told me that when Britain attacked Egypt she had painted the front door of our small house red. It felt good to be back.

In the following weeks I took to waving my arms and shouting about Suez. I shouted at a clergyman. I shouted at people in a greengrocer's in Hampstead Garden Suburb. I had been ashamed of England.

At about this time Jill and I had an evening in London. Afterwards we walked home from the Underground through the suburb; it was cold and misty under the flaring orange street lamps, which made our faces jaundiced and blotched with purple. We were happy and slightly tight, and we bobbled against each other as we walked.

Suddenly Jill said: 'I know you made love to two girls in Egypt. I just know it.'

'However did you know?' I asked.

'Oh!' said Jill. 'So you did.'

Part Four

In the early summer of 1957, the paper asked me to go to Algeria to write about the war that had already been going nearly three years.

'Write nothing while you're there,' the editor told me. 'Then come back here and take the lid off.'

There had been rumours that the French Army – particularly its parachutists – was not behaving well, though little was known of this in England at the time.

When I climbed from the airport bus in the centre of Algiers I saw leaning against a wall a fat, unshaven territorial (locally-recruited Home Guard), wearing dark glasses and smoking a cigarette. He was grasping a tommy-gun, and it didn't suit him.

The next day I collected my official press card from the Government buildings. An assistant press officer there, a kind man with prematurely grey hair and an odd, whimsical manner, drove me through splintering sunlight to his flat for a drink before lunch. The buildings of Algiers were tall and white; or tall and grey.

As we drank in the flat, we heard a baby crying upstairs.

'That baby and its mother are all alone at the moment,' said the press officer. 'The father, a teacher, was arrested by the parachutists, I think.'

He gave me a look.

'I don't know where he's gone,' he said.

That afternoon a captain from the parachute division in Algiers took me to see housing projects and welfare schemes that were designed to improve the lot of Muslims. The captain wore a green beret, which showed he was a parachutist of the Foreign Legion. Next he took me down the narrow main street of the Casbah, the walled Muslim quarter, a spidery hive of sand-coloured buildings. Armed parachutists were about; the Casbah did not seem lively. The captain took me into the garden of a small mosque: it was sprinkled with tombstones. He took a deep breath.

'It's peace here,' he said.

I liked him very much. He was tall, with fairish, cropped hair beneath his green beret, and a straight nose slightly turned up at the end. He seemed a quiet and honourable man; even a little monkish.

I made inquiries about the captain. He had been in Buchenwald during the war when very young for his part in the French Resistance. After that war he was in Indo-China for six years, fighting the Vietminh, who murdered his Indo-Chinese wife or mistress.

A day or two later the captain came to my hotel – it was like a Moorish palace, overlooking Algiers and the sea, and the door of my room had a brass plaque with upon it the name of my uncle, who had stayed in the room when the hotel was the headquarters of General Eisenhower during the war – and told me that General Massu, commanding the parachute division in Algiers, would see me.

We drove to Massu's divisional headquarters. We paused for a moment in the mess, which was neat and spare and, except for a faint smell of garlic, might have been a headquarters mess in the British Army. Then the captain took me into Massu.

The General was a tall, black-haired man of fifty, with a beaked nose, lowish forehead, and great physical strength. He wore a speckled brown-and-green parachutist's smock and powerful half-length boots. He had a wise smile and a likeable enough manner. When I asked him about the possibility of a military *coup d'état* in Algeria, he spoke of the French Army's tradition of loyalty to the Republic; but added that the Army could not allow a dishonourable solution: meaning, in effect, independence for Algeria, which he was unwilling to recognize as anything but defeat.

Massu felt like a man who, when he had made a decision, would grind it through. The concept of the honour and the glory of the French Army had formed his life. He personified the feeling among French officers that they were being sold by the politicians.

At that time I did not know of the methods of Massu's parachutists.

Edward, a colleague, then working for *Time Magazine*, and I took a train from Algiers to Oran. In the heat of summer the orange *bled* seemed to throb beneath a wrinkling heat haze as it rocked past the dusty windows of the train: it was burning, jaundiced, and it seemed to drive the gentlest men to thoughts of violence. The train was full of fat, blue-chinned young business-men in dark lightweight suits and yellow, ventilated shoes, with heavy black brief-cases, who in their conversation would suddenly explode with hatred against all Muslims. It was hard to like frightened men; I knew it in myself.

Edward and I went and had a drink in the refreshment car, whereupon someone must have tipped off the ticket collector about our unattended suitcases in the rack of our compartment. The collector hurried the length of the train, asking whose suit-cases these were, until at last he found us, and we said they were ours. He told us he was about to throw both suitcases out of the train, because he feared they might contain FLN bombs.

'I thought I heard one suitcase ticking,' he said.

After Oran, we travelled on to Tlemcen in French Army transport. On our first evening in Tlemcen, FLN terrorists, so it was said, opened fire on a mosque. Senegalese troops in sand-bagged positions fired wildly at any Muslim they saw; the uniformed territorials, all Europeans, did the same.

Because the firing continued, Edward and I wandered out to see what we could see. Blood lay on a long pavement not far from our hotel. Another fat, unshaven territorial, wearing dark glasses, surprisingly like the first I had seen in Algiers but this time a sergeant, and with his gaiters riding up his legs, swung his sub-machine-gun on us, and shouted to us to go back. It was as well neither of us looked much like a Muslim. We dodged into an open doorway, which turned out to be a mill. The owner of the mill, a solid and ironic-looking Jew, let us take shelter until the sergeant had lost interest in us.

'*Oh, les militaires, vous savez,*' said the Jew, with a shrug. 'What are they after in this life?'

When the firing had died a bit, Edward and I retreated from the mill towards our hotel. By now *tractions*, those famous black Citroëns used for years in every French gangster film, were rocketing past crammed with heavily-armed men in civilian clothes whose armaments bristled from the cars' windows. It seemed they were not satisfied with the number of Muslims slaughtered by the military. Fire-control did not look their strong point: every time a *traction* went past, we took cover as hastily as was decent behind the nearest plane tree.

At last the firing stopped. We returned to the hotel, whose young owner, originally a Parisian, was gibbering. He had recently had a grenade through one of the mosquito screens on his windows during a Saturday evening dance for soldiers and their girls. His nerves were poor. He showed us a loaded Colt he always kept handy. Then he opened the top drawer of the desk in his office leading off the hall, and pulled out a string of grenades, all primed. His hands were shaking.

'One can't be too ready,' he said.

I sent a postcard from Tlemcen to my editor: it was the only one I could find on an old Arab's stall; it was of a small white kitten with pink glass eyes, whose slightly convex cardboard stomach squeaked when you pressed it.

We left Tlemcen feeling depressed. For a day or two we toured the 'pacified' *bled* of Western Algeria with a charming middle-aged French major, recalled from the reserve, and an armed escort. In each *commune* the bedrock of the campaign of 'pacification' was usually a French officer in a blue *képi*. He had a little post in the *bled*, in the brown and bony hills, with a detachment of Muslim auxiliary policemen, and an office usually bare except for a stirring painting of some scene from the First World War.

At one point, looking at a map, we asked to be driven to a lonely village in the hills some way from the main road. This, as far as the French were concerned, was unlikely to be a show village for journalists. The major did not seem keen to take us. We insisted. At last, in two vehicles, our truck and its escort, we ground up a grass-and-gravel track for some kilometres, with, on either side, high red-earth banks and scrub ideal for an ambush. Did the major look uneasy? We reached the village, which was of small mud houses and, at first glance, uninhabited. Then we saw a few old bearded men and young boys, almost all in rags. Where were the rest? Had the women and children been removed to those fortified compounds run by the French Army, so that they would be powerless to succour the rebels? Where were the men of military age: with the FLN? with the French Army? Slaughtered? This village, which was Berber, had an air of having known sad and violent days. A fair-skinned boy of about fifteen with a turban and worn blue pantaloons walked into the village while we were there with a strange, peg-legged gait, carrying over his shoulder a primitive wooden hoe. He passed the armed French soldiers with a distant smile on his face.

An American professor and I were sitting in a pavement café in Algiers on a fine Sunday evening in June when cars full of young people went by fast, blasting their horns and overtaking. They kept their horns going till they were out of sight.

'A wedding,' said the professor.

But there were ambulances. Not long afterwards we heard that a bomb had exploded during a tea-dance in the Casino de la Corniche in St Eugene, a suburb of Algiers. The people we saw were the lucky ones, going home.

It was just dark when we got there, warm, with mad clouds and a watery moon. A police wagon was drawn up outside the Casino, and *flics* with sub-machine-guns stood about.

'You can't go in,' they said.

They had blue chins and *képis*. They looked like Corsicans. We talked while we waited for the officer.

'*Ce n'est pas très gai,*' said one of the policemen. 'Young people. What had they done?'

There wasn't much to say. The marble steps looked, at a quick glance, pretty muddy.

'*Ce n'est pas du sang?*' asked an American journalist.

It was more a thought; he hadn't really meant to say it aloud.

'*Ce n'est pas du vin rouge, monsieur,*' replied the policeman.

An officer appeared at the door. He was quite young, in plain-clothes, and, it seemed, senior. He had telephoned higher authority. We could go in after all.

It was a plushy, shiny place. Debris and glass from mirrors lay on the red carpet in the long hall. We paused on the two steps leading to the tables and the dance floor. The time-bomb had exploded against the orchestra platform while they were playing something South American; the blast had annihilated the band leader and cut into the dancers. The bloody violence accentuated the frivolous décor. A young woman's foot was all by itself in a fashionable shoe. A waiter was explaining something to the police. A colonel wearing civilian clothes and with a black leather band across an old wound on his nose thought it was a plastic bomb.

'They're getting very strong in this line now,' said a policeman.

As we left the proprietor was gesticulating hopelessly: 'One can't stay in this country, one can't stay,' he kept repeating.

The funeral of the victims was two days later. The newspapers of Algiers had details of the funeral routes; people said there was going to be trouble; there was an inevitability about their attitude. The *Anciens Combattants* and student organizations (one of them receiving a handsome subsidy from M. Robert Lacoste, the Minister Resident, a Socialist) had time to lay their plans and had called a strike to show their 'grief and anger'.

Early on the day of the funeral, about a dozen students and a handful of toughish-looking men of between thirty and forty, some of them in shorts, gathered near a hospital in the centre of Algiers from which the corpses were to be borne. It was a leaden day. A jet helicopter kept circling the area. The students and veterans went round European shops and banks, ordering them to close. They began to chase buses and to smash the windows if they didn't stop or were carrying Muslims.

'Don't stand about,' screamed one of the older ringleaders to Europeans in the street. 'We don't want spectators. Join us, you who are good Frenchmen.'

The 10th Parachute Division, commanded by General Massu, had returned to Algiers following the bomb outrages, and European families standing on balconies cheered and clapped as a section went past in jeeps. The students and the *Anciens Combat-*

tants went on up the street, shouting to people to join them. Police stood about watching; it was hard to understand why they didn't arrest the ringleaders; two or three hours' cooling off in a cell would have been sufficient.

Farther up, a young Arab with a badly cut face was led away by friends. A photographer who had had his camera smashed when trying to photograph the burning of an Arab's motor-bike was looking glum. Two European women were bending over something in the shade of a tree on the pavement; they looked worried: it was a small black kitten, helpless, its eyes not yet open.

The jet helicopter was circling towards us; and then, when it had passed, we heard: the 'Marseillaise'. Several hundred students came in sight, marching ten abreast. A large, dark European stepped out of an arcade of shops to watch them coming up the street.

'They're marvellous, those *gosses*,' he said. 'And it's entirely spontaneous.'

He deceived himself: ringleaders were noticeable in the front rank. In a square they broke and chased a young Arab. His mother, wizened and without a veil, screamed at them. They overturned a couple of cars belonging to Muslims (owners' names were written on windscreens, by order). We were now in the Bab-el-Oued quarter, where Muslims, Jews and Europeans of French, Spanish, Maltese and Italian descent all lived together in high tenement houses, and from which came several victims of the Casino bomb.

'We don't want *L'Express* or *France-Observateur* here today,' shouted some rowdies behind us.

Both these newspapers were hated for their critical attitude to French policy in Algeria by most of the European population. Some young reporters from local newspapers moved away from us discreetly. Perhaps they thought we were unsafe company. Families stared down from balconies. More people were joining the throng.

'I don't know whether I can come or not,' puffed an old Spanish-looking woman, dressed in black.

'Well, don't if you don't want to,' said someone who must have been her daughter.

A group of giggling girls blocked the path of an Army lorry. The mob clambered up a bank, heading for a miserable *bidonville* that lay alongside a fine new block of flats. They overturned a car in the *bidonville*, set light to its petrol-tank and tried to make the flames spread to the Muslims' shacks, which they also stoned. Robed Muslim women who lived there attempted to hurl stones back. Their men had gone into the Casbah, in order to make a resistance if the Casbah were attacked in force.

On the road above, a Spahi captain, elderly, with a good face, managed to disarm a few of the youths carrying splintered staves. He was one of the very few soldiers to do anything good that day. The mob burnt out another *bidonville* and severely beat an old Arab whom they caught on the road. He looked as though he might have had a fractured skull, and was later dumped in the back of a jeep by soldiers.

'Do you think this is worthwhile?' we asked a tall and attractive Corsican girl in a white dress who was following the throng.

'No,' she said. 'It's not. We're sheep. We follow.'

After the mob had done its work, police appeared and made a show of dispersing them.

'You know, we have to let the young let off steam,' said a police officer with a sheepish grin. 'They have a great anger after the bombs. It's understandable. You English will understand after your troubles in Palestine.'

The young didn't seem angry to us; they were enjoying themselves.

'We have no orders,' said another officer.

The mob headed back to the centre of Algiers, where cars collected them for lunch. It was organized. Farther on they were still at it: sacking Muslim shops and cafés, aided by uniformed territorials, one of whom broke off his work for a moment to fire his automatic pistol wildly through a barbed-wire barricade into the Casbah. They smashed the metal blinds of closed shops with chairs and benches. They tore and slashed the contents into small pieces: men's clothes, scent, groceries. Devastation was complete. After breaking and burning a few more motor-bikes, they, too, went in for lunch.

One attractive, dark-haired girl, a ringleader, lived near by; her elderly mother came out to meet her, and the girl, bright-eyed and wild, laughingly told of the morning's work. It had been a successful exercise. The funerals were not until the afternoon, when there would be the real business of the day.

The professor and I lunched that day just inside the Casbah, where it was quiet, the quietest place in all Algiers, though it was reputed to be dangerous. Young men in dark suits came into the small Arab restaurant once or twice to look at us; wherever we went in the Casbah we found we were discreetly inspected. By the FLN? By Lacoste's men? We never knew.

There were large crowds in Bab-el-Oued after lunch. The ringleaders were arriving on scooters, girl-friends sitting behind carrying *tricolores* and wearing, this time, not dresses, but jeans: they were serious now. They began smashing up Arab shops, the crowds screaming and cheering.

'There'll be blood flowing this afternoon,' cried a square Frenchman. 'There'll be blood. You'll see. English and American, are you? I was in Italy under General Mark Clark, General Clark, a great general; the greatest. Look at them there, it's down in the Casbah they should be attacking. You can't treat the Arabs like you would another race; they're a race apart; you can't understand.'

They systematically picked out every Arab shop in the area, smashing in the closed metal blinds and burning the contents; they burnt Muslims' stalls from two communal markets; threw into the air rubber balls from a toyshop, which powerful women in black grasped for their grandchildren; hurled live chickens to one another until the birds had lost their feathers and then trampled them to death.

'Spare animals,' cried one small, grey-haired man.

He was disregarded.

They broke and emptied the tanks of motor-bikes over meat torn from butchers, set fire to the petrol that soaked the carcasses, and armed themselves with the meat-hooks.

'Those meat-hooks are bound to be used on somebody before the day's over,' said the professor.

Streets ran with milk and broken eggs; the mob pawed and stamped the debris like animals and poured wine over one another's heads (would a Muslim have stocked alcohol, or had they for once mistaken a shop's identity?).

'See, they never steal,' exclaimed a man proudly.

It was almost true. But now and again, mothers, instead of themselves taking cigarettes, guiltily stuffed the packets into the pockets of their small children.

Police, firemen and security troops of the Ministry of the Interior, wearing large black helmets, arrived always when things were over, to make a show of cordoning off the gutted shop or of squirting water on the charred remains. As the operation got under way, paratroops took to shutting off each street that was being sacked, keeping out spectators, but allowing the gangs to work their way systematically through the Arab shops.

Early on, the biggest crowd was in a wide street, milling about with territorials at their head. Men in black suits and dark glasses were giving orders. They looked very much like plain-clothes police officers from Paris, which was perhaps the effect they sought: one, when questioned, said he was a stranger to the area. A captain of *gendarmerie* rode about standing up in a jeep, waving his arms and declaiming, although it was hard to say whether he was actually helping to organize the riot or had been overcome by excitement. The leaders in dark glasses then ordered the crowd, with its spearhead of territorials, to advance upon a cordon of parachutists. There was a little mock clash, apparently prearranged, like something out of pantomime.

'*Massu au pouvoir, Massu au pouvoir*,' chanted the crowd.

Sometimes they chanted, '*Soustelle au pouvoir*.'

Next, a captain of parachutists read out a proclamation from a loudspeaker truck with such *panache* and *élan* (the 'glory' and 'honour' of the French Army came into it continuously, together with the name of General Massu) that we thought we were watching a *coup d'état*. (But this didn't actually happen until a year later.)

When we asked for the text of the captain's proclamation, which was written on a scrap of paper, a rather tough man who behaved like an *agent provocateur* '('if you're American I advise you to be careful: we know journalists, bad journalists, bad, we want good journalists' – all this accompanied by a finger stabbing my chest) shouted to the soldiers not to give it to us.

Eventually we were told it was no more than a proclamation from General Massu telling the people to go home quietly. No one took it seriously and the parachutists made no attempt to enforce it.

We pushed our way through the crowd to the church where the funeral services were being held. A coffin appeared, draped in a black cloth adorned with a silver cross and carried by territorials, the unhappy family of the dead person walking behind; organization seemed entirely in the hands of the territorials, one of them marching at the head of the procession, puffed up, wrist cocked, shouting orders, a Fascist incarnate.

The main crowd was not interested in the funeral. It was going through the houses, pulling out Arab men who had not taken refuge in the Casbah. One fat old Arab in blue denims, horribly beaten, staggered off, gasping with terror; another, much younger, his skull smashed, was dragged away and flung dead into the back of an Army truck. Those were Arabs, perhaps small shopkeepers, who had chosen to live in a European quarter, and must have been well known to many of the rioters. Among the crowd were smartly-dressed men and women spectators, bright-eyed, watching as though it were a point-to-point. Girls and boys in the mob sometimes embraced after the boy concerned had done something particularly savage. Whenever we asked a question, the attitude was always the same: 'They're not like another race, the Muslims. They've really overdone it, you see. Savages. Young girls with their legs amputated from that bomb in the Casino.'

Even a friendly-looking dressmaker and her grown-up daughter (who had appalling toothache, her jaw swaddled in bandages) felt the same. We stopped at the window of their apartment to ask them for a glass of water, hoping they were not infected with the madness. But everyone in Bab-el-Oued was quite willing to accept that it was right and proper to take revenge on any Muslim, however innocent.

When the orgy was at its height, there were bursts of sub-machine-gun fire. A terribly injured European woman (who died soon afterwards) and two or three others with nasty injuries were carried through the wailing crowd to cars. At first we thought they had gunshot wounds. Then we saw a large truck jammed against the wall of a narrow side-street. It must have run into the crowd. A paratrooper leant over a parapet with his sub-machine-gun and fired a long burst into the head and body of the Arab driver, who had been pulled out of his cab. The crowd, pointing to the load in the back of the truck, were screaming 'Search the straw, there may be a bomb.' By this time they did really seem to think the driver was a terrorist. He was a fat-faced young Muslim with a big moustache, who had driven into Bab-el-Oued unaware, presumably, of the riots; he had become frightened, had charged a line of parachutists and, almost certainly wounded by the first burst of fire, had crushed several people.

The paratrooper who had shot him climbed down from the parapet and, after an interval of some minutes, fired three or four more bursts into the head of the driver, who must have been already dead. There was a long 'Aaaaaahhh' from the crowd. The paratrooper was young with a pale face: later, he touched me, and smiled, when he was moving the crowd in order that the young civilian killers could do their work more easily. His hand was cold.

They used the meat-hooks: they were bound to. The victim was another young Muslim in blue denims lying face down in the road; he must have been the truck-driver's mate, and he was dead. It seemed that there was some power at work outside the control of human beings.

'C'est écœurant' ('sickening'), said another young paratrooper. He was one of the very few people that I heard express regret that day.

The passive complicity of the police and soldiers was the most frightening thing. They did almost nothing to prevent the slaughter and destruction, although there were thousands of them in Algiers. A battalion of good troops armed not with sub-machine-guns but with clubs could have stopped the worst disturbances. If they had arrested twenty ringleaders early in the morning there would have been no riots at all. Were they afraid to take action against Europeans?

They said M. Lacoste banged the table in anger when he heard what had happened. But he must have known what was in the wind. Everyone else in Algiers seemed to know. Lacoste had power to give orders to the police, who appeared to have no orders. General Massu, commanding the Algiers area, could have done what he liked with the military.

'We're afraid of being abandoned by France, so we've got to show how we feel,' was the argument of the more sane Frenchmen of Algiers to justify the day.

Two hundred rioters were arrested, but only four were detained.

'Let them go, let them go,' the mob yelled.

The police and CRS meekly obeyed.

Walking back through the town, past the skeletons of burnt cars, the air was heavy. It was cooler by the sea, and the evening was fine.

'I don't think I like human beings,' said the professor. 'I've seen some things, but nothing like that. It ought to be a warning to people of what's happening here. Few people took much notice of the symptoms in Germany before the war.'

A long column of armoured cars was moving into the centre of Algiers. Whom had they come to protect, and against what?

Night came fast. Curfew was at nine, instead of the usual hour of midnight. We hurried back to our hotels on foot, since all transport was included in the strike. Mobile columns of parachutists waited in their trucks and jeeps: in the dusk in their speckled smocks and peaked fatigue caps, they looked in some curious way like Japanese soldiers.

A girl journalist said that night, 'I saw the Muslim truck-driver after he'd been shot on the ground. There was a rose by his head.'

That night in my hotel a large party ate at the table next to mine. All the waiters were Algerian Muslims. I could never forget the hands of the expensively-dressed Frenchwomen eating there: brown carmine-nailed talons, beneath gold bracelets, picking at the rich food.

A day or two later, we went to the Palais de Justice to hear the case against the four arrested rioters, but were directed from one floor to another.

An angry chief clerk said: 'I don't know anything of the case you're interested in. But you would do better to occupy yourselves writing about what happened in the Casino at St Eugene on Sunday night. Yesterday they buried a coffer of human remains.'

We learnt that two of the four rioters were in 'provisional liberty'.

A French journalist said: 'I heard from a colleague you were making inquiries at the Palais de Justice. They'll let the other two go when foreign journalists are no longer showing interest.'

I wrote a full account of the riot in the paper. Yet the putsches, and, four or five years later, the murderous doings of the OAS, caused surprise.

A few weeks later, two thousand French troops, using artillery, tanks, and air support, surrounded two hundred and ten young Algerians, armed only with old rifles, on a bony plateau in Eastern Algeria. The battle lasted nearly two days. Two hundred and five of the two hundred and ten young Algerians died. The French took five prisoners of nineteen or twenty years old. They interrogated them and showed them off to journalists and photographers. Then they stood them, bareheaded and back to back, in a truck, and paraded them through the streets of Tebessa, while loudspeakers played 'Madelon'. It was a curious spectacle that would not have seemed out of place to those former governors of Tebessa, the Romans. While 'Madelon' played and the five young Algerian prisoners, heads unbowed, were shown off to the populace, old Arabs in the cafés bent over their coffee with impassive faces that never looked up. Afterwards we lunched in the officers' mess of the French parachutist regiment that had taken a leading part in the action; the regiment had had one or two young officers and other ranks killed. The officers in the mess were in great form, laughing uproariously with a couple of French Army nurses. The padre ordered champagne.

A few days after that, a young Algerian working in Algiers Radio drove round and round Algiers for hours in his small car. French parachutists had just arrested three of his colleagues.

'What's happening to them?' he kept repeating. 'That's what I want to know.'

He knew; and he knew he might be next. A Roman Catholic chaplain in the parachute division had already attempted to justify torture in the search for nationalist terrorists, and had backed his argument by scripture.

Torture with a magneto was not the only method used. Victims were pumped full of water, pressure being supplied by a small motor.

'When they jump on you afterwards, that's not so amusing,' said the grey-haired Frenchman who worked as a press officer in the Government buildings. 'Something may give.'

There was the cold bath; there was the hanging of naked victims upside down and right way up, apart from the other less official refinements, such as the use of bottles on girls. The FLN later showed me men with what I was told, and believed, were electrode burns on tongue, ear, and cock. I saw a street vendor from a village near Tebessa who, arms tied behind his back, had been hung up by his wrists for a day and a half, although he was cut down at night. Muscles and nerves in his arms and shoulders had gone, he was paralysed in the upper body, and could not feed himself. The man said his captors asked no questions, which showed that once torture for information was accepted, gratuitous brutality soon followed. He said that twenty-five of thirty-six men rounded up with him were later shot. It was not hard to learn of these things in Algeria.

The American professor wanted to go right into the Casbah of Algiers itself to find out what was really going on there. The prospect scared me a bit, since French officers had told me that to go into the hive of the Casbah was dangerous because of terrorists; journalists were not going in then. But the professor, who had just recovered from a serious operation, had no fear. 'Put on a dark, unobtrusive shirt,' he said, 'and we'll go in.'

So we did. The Casbah was another world, apart. In a side-street one of our first acts was to buy some yellow-and-black artificial silk from a lame man spinning it in a little alcove that was scarcely more than a groove in a wall by running water. He could not get real silk.

'Give my regards to President Eisenhower and Mr Macmillan,' said the spinner of silk, on learning our nationalities.

'We're in a cage,' a Muslim said on our next visit, when we found ourselves up against one of the barriers of barbed wire that blocked the narrow streets. Comparison with a ghetto was easy.

On our visits to the Casbah we heard countless tales of the arrest of Muslims, their families having no idea where they had been taken. A typical story was the arrest of a boy of seventeen who was supporting his mother and young brothers because his father was dead, shot by the FLN, who mistook him for a European. His mother protested to the soldiers before they took him away, and begged them to release him.

'What does it matter to me what happens to your son?' said a young French parachutist. 'I'll shoot your whole family like mine was shot by the Germans.'

The German occupation of France may have had some bearing on the Algerian tragedy. I thought how little England had known of this European experience, and how extremely lucky and sheltered we had been.

For more than a week after the arrest of this Algerian boy, his mother went from one authority to another, seeking news of him.

'*Allez, allez,*' they told her, or: 'It's not this office you want.'

The mother was normally jolly and plump, and wore, when at home, pantaloons and no veil.

We quite often visited two Muslim acquaintances who worked for the Algiers municipality. One evening the young man opened the door. He had a moustache, and could have been taken for a Spaniard. This time he looked green.

'Something bad's happened,' he said. 'Come in. My friend was arrested last night. The paras, a policeman, and a man in civilian clothes. I don't know where they've taken him.'

We could hear the sounds of the arrested man's children playing upstairs.

'The children will be all right,' his friend said. 'There's no trouble about money for him, luckily. But what's happened to him? Mind you, in a way it would be a relief to be arrested. It would be over, the uncertainty. Here in the Casbah we're the reprieved dead.'

We asked about some visits we had earlier arranged to make with him that evening.

'Look,' he said. 'I'm a bit shocked by this arrest. Forgive me. He's my best friend. I had wanted to take you to meet some people. But now . . .'

'You'd rather we didn't come any more?' we asked.

'Well, forgive me. You understand? Even being seen in the Casbah with a European can be difficult. The police or CRS turn round and look at you. And then, you never know . . .'

'You could be arrested just for being with us?'

'It's possible.'

We felt we had better say good-bye and not come again.

'Tell them in your papers,' he said, 'that the Arabs are hungry, not so much for bread but for liberty.'

His dark eyes flashed and his moustache twitched and he looked more than ever like a Spaniard. We never saw him again.

People were disappearing without trace in Algiers then, having died of torture or been shot because too disfigured to return to the light of day. A note might announce that they were 'shot while trying to escape', had 'escaped', or had 'committed suicide'. Muslims said that the 'Green Berets', the parachutists of the Foreign Legion, were the worst torturers, and that there was one special German group working in the Casbah.

Not long before I left, the press officer of the Parachute Division, the captain in the 'Green Berets' who had taken me to see General Massu, came one evening for a drink in my hotel. With his brick-coloured face, big boots, and parachutist's smock, he seemed out of place in the flashy bar.

The barman was a rabid Arab-hater. Whenever I remonstrated with him he hissed with rage and venom. He was frightened.

On this evening, the captain, as he drank whisky, said that the German element in the Foreign Legion was 'not more than about sixty per cent of the total', and that few of the Germans, despite rumours, were ex-SS men.

'We like our Germans, don't we?' he said with a smile to the barman.

The barman winked.

I asked the captain the difference between what the French parachutists were doing in Algeria and what the Germans had done in the war.

'Well,' he said. 'The Germans did things coldly, systematically.'

The captain told me he thought it noble to die for a hopeless cause; 'or for nothing'.

Back in England it was hard to explain to people what it was like in Algeria. To forget it, I took to flying kites: gazing up into the sun and feeling the pull of the wind.

A kite is relaxing. People in the East know this, particularly the Chinese, who send up into the sky on their kites beautiful messages – often to God.

Kites get some people so that they can think of little else; it is something to do with the desire to climb higher. In India, during festivals, children become so absorbed in their kites that they fall off roofs while flying them. My brother Adrian once lost a giant kite high over the Dorset coast: he followed it in a fishing-boat, broke an oar, and had to swim more than a mile back to land on a November day.

The record height for a kite is about four and a half miles – probably with about nine miles of string, piano wire or nylon thread and with several kites flown in series one above the other: when one kite ceases to climb, and the line curves excessively, you release another.

W. G. Grace's father (or it may have been grandfather) was a considerable kite-flyer: he once drove a kite-drawn carriage from Bristol to London; on another occasion he suspended his wife with box kites above the Cheddar Gorge. Yet kites are essentially peaceful, and the flying of them is a philosophical exercise, a bit like yoga.

I used hexagonal plastic kites, with tails that I lengthened, depending on the strength of the wind. Often I flew three in series, to a height of about 1,500 feet. In warm weather they would climb in almost still air. My line was mainly of Italian hemp, on a winder turned by a bicycle pedal.

There are few things more satisfactory than kites swimming in a fine evening sky and flicking their tails; and nothing can seem higher than a high kite, even in these days – it is a kind of restricted ultimate, and in imagining yourself up with the kite, you feel wonderful. There is skill in flying kites from a tree-lined garden: it combines science with the mystery of fishing.

I took seriously to kite-flying when I lost the kite of my son, James, then aged three. It broke away and floated into the dusk, eventually catching its string in a tall poplar in the garden of a supposed millionaire near our suburb. The garden's wrought-iron gates were barred; no one answered the bell. It grew dark and began to rain. People going to a synagogue opposite were very sympathetic when they caught sight of the kite against a light patch in the sky, and they stopped momentarily to discuss it, and to wonder where the millionaire and his retainers were.

This kite was only of paper, and it rustled almost inaudibly in the darkness and the rain until we saw it no more. Next morning it had disappeared. I thought James was upset, and got him another, larger one, made of plastic. Then it turned out he was not interested in kites at all, except when they towed a four-wheeled horse, which leaked straw, across a playing-field.

The best kite-flyers fly their kites with the line always near breaking point; it is almost intoxicating. When they get them to the right height, they tether them all night to a stake or an apple tree.

One evening I overdid it near Ashdown Forest: the line broke and two red kites escaped into the sunset. More than a mile of Italian hemp came down in the tops of trees, across telephone wires and over roofs. My brother-in-law and I hauled most of it in, and in the clear air we heard people exclaiming at the strange whistling noise as the line passed over their rooftops. Then it broke again, and we traced it to a field of grotesque roots, inhabited by pigs.

An Italian peasant girl, strong and bow-legged in a red dress, came out and watched us groping for the line among the roots. She worked for the smallholder who owned the pigs, had been left in charge that night, and wasn't sure what we were up to.

At last we untangled the line from the roots, found the two

kites intact in the middle of a magnificent ploughed field, and drove home in our van feeling we had accomplished something.

I thought I had finished with Algeria; but I had not. In November 1957, six months before de Gaulle came back to power, when France, it seemed, might have gone Fascist or have known civil war as a consequence of the war in Algeria, the paper sent me to Paris to write about what I saw and heard. At least five hundred people had been assassinated there in the past few months: mainly Algerians by Algerians, as a result, it was said, of nationalist rivalry; but Europeans with important Algerian connexions had been shot at, too; so had Frenchmen who disliked the continuation of the Algerian war and the activities of the French right-wing; liberal and left-wing journalists were unpopular.

One of the worst killings then was in an Algerians' dormitory in the Paris suburb of Bondy, a raw place of red brick buildings under cold skies. The dormitory was above a shop with a closed metal blind. The exaggerated shadows of Algerians moved about in the pale electric light behind lace curtains. A charred creeper clung to the wall. The Algerians in Paris, many of them living in miserable *bidonvilles* on the outskirts of the city, had often a hunted, shamefaced look. With their berets very straight on their heads, they might look over their shoulders for an instant as they held swing doors for you when you left the Métro. The police could arrest and detain anyone they thought dangerous for up to twenty-one days before committing him to a magistrate, and what went on when the man was in police hands was anyone's guess.

One of the several Parisians with an unofficial bodyguard at this time was Maître Jean Baptiste Biaggi, leader of the recently-formed para-military Patriotic Revolutionary Party, which was dedicated to French nationalism and the taking of power by 'the methods that seem most necessary'. He was a roly-poly Corsican lawyer (once de Gaulle's) with glasses and an uncontrolled laugh. By now most of his clients were French mobsters in Algeria, who got away with murder. Biaggi's bodyguard, a square young Corsican with dark hair growing far down a low brow, was known as 'the Black Angel', and had a reputation for trigger-happiness and killing. When Biaggi had formed his party, two weeks before I was sent to Paris, a journalist had asked, 'Are you Fascist?' Biaggi said no, Fascism was against the spirit of France.

Biaggi and the militia he was allowed to command had already played a part in the Algerian violence before he formed them into a 'party'. It was he who had organized the tomato-throwing, spitting, and Arab-chasing for Guy Mollet's visit to Algiers in February 1956, when that French socialist Premier lost his nerve trying to reach an agreement with the Algerian nationalists. As a result, the Algerian war dragged on for another six years.

In Paris Biaggi lived in a magnificent apartment lined with light-oak mock-eighteenth-century bookcases and reached by way of red carpeted stairs below large mirrors. There Biaggi had seventeen busts of a fellow Corsican, Napoleon. Many of Biaggi's followers were Corsicans. Biaggi was plump, short and dark, with horn-rimmed glasses and large hands; he would not have looked out of place on the nineteenth hole of an English suburban golf course. He had much charm at first, and a tendency to pat one's knee and look like a spaniel seeking approval. He told malicious stories about a respected French Minister at that time, who, according to Biaggi, was 'a secret agent of the Cocos' (Communists).

Biaggi's theory was that France was the 'Anglo-Saxon sputnik', her Government was 'less free than the Czech Government at Munich'. The dollar occupation was 'less visible than the German helmet' in the last war, but the same thing. M. Gaillard, then Premier, was, he thought, less of a nationalist than Marshal Pétain; he was influenced by Jean Monnet, who, Biaggi said, was 'an American agent'. Biaggi at this time was getting a lot of fun from actions such as the breaking-up of the political meetings of M. Mendès-France with tear gas and ex-parachutists who infiltrated the ranks of the Mendèsist chuckers-out.

Biaggi asked a professorial-looking Swiss journalist and me out to lunch. When we came out of Biaggi's big apartment house, 'the Black Angel' was keeping an eye on the windows opposite and on the occupants of cars: all must have seemed well, and we went round the corner to the Peugeot with 'the Black Angel' out in front at a slow lope, his automatic showing in his raincoat. We were off to Fred's, 'the best bistro in Paris' according to Biaggi.

At Fred's, Biaggi would not admit Algerian nationalism: every sort of nationalisn bar that, it seemed. He spoke of people in France he claimed were 'corrupt and traitorous'. He admired Sir Winston Churchill and Aneurin Bevan – but not apparently Lord Altrincham, who had recently had his face slapped for his remarks about the Queen. Biaggi said he was against torture in Algeria; his followers had been known to say there was not enough. He thought Frenchmen might be shooting Americans in French streets within five years, 'although I'm against it personally'. He felt his day would come ('I'll use the methods that seem most necessary at the time') when social unrest in France grew really serious. He walked about in the *bistro,* served us himself, spearing a great loaf of *pâté* on a long knife, ordered us blue steak three inches thick, and quoted Prince Hal after the death of Hotspur superbly, in glowing French, to show his 'belief in man'.

Biaggi was reputed to have fought bravely in the French Resistance. It was hard to take him seriously, until you remembered he had been giggling about stripping Muslim village girls naked and making them dance.

After reporting Biaggi's doings and the atmosphere in Paris that November, the paper asked me to stay on in Paris and write a profile of M. Robert Lacoste, that old Socialist, then still Minister Resident in Algeria. Lacoste, the Socialist, and Biaggi, the right-winger, had something in common. Lacoste, too, had played a big part in the wartime Resistance; it seemed hard to find a Frenchman who had not. Robert Lacoste, 'Bob' to his friends, was a short, round man, with powerful arms, big head, well-nourished features, and a wisecracking manner. He had been schoolmaster and union boss. He had quick darting eyes and liked to get a laugh. At times he could be silken.

Despite his glory as French proconsul in Algeria, he sometimes let it be known, with a wink and a chuckle, that he was really more at home in shirtsleeves, eating fish soup in a *bistro*. When I had visited him once in his headquarters in a Moorish palace in Algiers, he told me: 'Believe me, Monsieur Gale, this is a terrible job. Terrible. You can't imagine what a terrible job it is.' His voice quavered and he hid his head in his hands, looking as though he might cry. I couldn't decide whether this was put on for my benefit. When I left his office, there were some terrible-looking men outside the door.

In public Lacoste was well-known for his cracks about the Americans and their appetite for oil; about what a terrible, hopeless job it was to be French Premier; about what the British did to the Kikuyu in Kenya, or what the Americans did to the Red Indians and were still doing to the Negroes in the Deep South. He had a big, laughing mouth, and sometimes bent his knees and gestured like a jockey coming up to the finishing post. When he was criticized for his talk of 'the last quarter of an hour', of the imminent end of the Algerian rebellion (five years before it did end) he would say: 'I remember old Clemenceau in 1918, when I was in Champagne, saying, "Hold!" And little did I think then that the end was so near.'

A minority of French Socialists said that Lacoste was betraying Socialism. Some people described him as 'the prisoner of the Government General', with a large staff between himself and the realities of the Algerian crisis. Others said he was powerless in face of the generals and the Army, or that he had been won over by the 'ultras', the diehard right-wing settlers. Thus, privately, the Minister Resident would hold his head in his hands and say he'd give anything to change his job; publicly he was given to statements like '*J'y suis, J'y reste*'('I'm here and I'll stay').

M. Lacoste was a hard man to pin down. An Italian journalist once asked him, 'Can you tell me, Mr Minister, the difference between your "pacification" and war?' Lacoste's first reaction was to make a joke in an Italian accent, which got him a big laugh from local journalists standing near by. Then he added: 'I'll let you have transport and facilities to travel where you like in Algeria for six months, if, at the end of that time, you can come to me and give me in fifteen lines a true definition of the word "pacification".'

Five years before peace came in Algeria, a good Frenchman told me that one of the greatest obstacles to peace and independence for Algeria was the arming of not only the European territorials and other auxiliaries, but of almost all European civilians.

161

The arming of Europeans greatly increased after Lacoste took office. In Algiers I heard a story about a Muslim who had been shot by onlookers as he tried to escape after a supposed terrorist attack in the city. When they picked him up dead off the pavement, he turned out to be not a Muslim but a Frenchman: there were, the story went, thirty-two different calibres of bullet in his body.

That week in Paris I set about gathering material for the profile of Lacoste, who was in Paris at the time, having flown from Algiers for a big debate on the Algerian war. The delightful girl who was secretary of the paper's Paris office went, as a result of a misunderstanding, to the Algeria office in Paris to collect material on Lacoste, and mentioned that I was in Paris to write the profile. The series I had written on the Algerian war some months earlier had not been popular with the French authorities in Algiers.

'Monsieur Gale is imaginative,' Lacoste's press officer said to the girl. 'We wonder if he was paid in roubles or pounds sterling.'

When the girl protested, the Press Officer retracted, but with ill grace, and then took her in to see Lacoste: the Minister was shaving. She came back and told me what had happened.

I took out the series I had written on Algeria, and read through it to see if I could find anything that had since been proved wrong or unfair. I could not. I decided to go round to see the press officer, taking my series with me, and to ask him to dispute what I had written.

I walked out of the paper's Paris office, taking with me the series and a notebook in which to take down the press officer's words, since they might well provide material for the profile of Lacoste. My Biro had run out, so I went into a near-by Prisunic to buy another. Two Algerians, standing about near the entrance to the office, followed me into the Prisunic, and, as I was choosing a Biro (it was, I think, actually a Bic), they nudged me, and held out a piece of paper on which something was written. One of the Algerians seemed to be clearly an Arab, the other a Berber. What did they want with me? In North Africa I knew the leaders of the FLN, but I had no great wish to make contact at this time with the FLN in Paris; nor did it seem wise. I knew most of what

I needed to know about the Algerian tragedy, and had written of it. Why were those Algerians nudging me, and what was their message? I ignored them. I paid and walked out of the Prisunic. I knew that at this time there were plenty of Algerians in French employ for reasons not always wholesome. The French authorities then were keen to discredit critics of their Algerian policies: funny things had happened to some people.

Feeling that I was perhaps being absurd, I walked quickly from the Prisunic and, beneath a railway viaduct, hailed a taxi and asked the driver to take me to the Algeria Office, where I hoped to find Lacoste's press officer and even Lacoste himself. When I got there I found neither was available, since both were listening to the debate on Algeria. Not certain whether to try again later, and having nothing to do, I walked a few paces round the corner to a café and bar called the Dauphine, a well-known meeting-place for politicians and journalists.

It was about four o'clock. I ordered a coffee at the bar, which was empty. Soon five men entered. Their leader, for such he seemed to be, had silver hair and wore a camel-hair overcoat. I did not much care for the look of the five men, who went to a table in the shadow of a corner, where they ordered nothing. After a time the silver-haired one went over to the far side of the curved bar, opposite me. He told the girl at the switchboard near the bar to get him a number, and took the call there, instead of going downstairs to use the telephone in one of the kiosks in the basement; he spoke rapidly, occasionally looking across sideways towards me.

'Yes, he's here,' I heard him say.

I asked the barman for a *jeton*, and went downstairs to the public telephones. To my surprise, the five men came down into the basement after me. All, except the silver-haired one, had fawn raincoats. I went into the nearest telephone kiosk, and the five men went into the lavatory, the door of which was immediately opposite. I looked up the number of the British Embassy in the directory, but took some time, since I had forgotten it was under '*Royaume Uni*'. As I was searching for the number, with the door of the telephone kiosk open, each one of the men, except their leader, came out in turn from the lavatory and stood right against the kiosk, without saying anything, and each had his right hand in the pocket of his raincoat. Who were they? I had seen too much easy killing in Algeria to feel at ease. The killing was spreading to France. I found the number of the Embassy at last, and got through to someone who had been helpful to me before I had first gone to Algeria.

'Hullo,' I said. 'It's John Gale here. How are you? Sorry to bother you. I wonder if I could come round and see you?'

'By all means.'

'By the way . . .'

'Yes?'

'You may think this is a bit odd. But I'm telephoning you from the basement of the Dauphine. You know, the café at the north end of the Boulevard St Germain. Well, there are some rather odd people down in this basement where I'm telephoning, and I don't feel too happy. They look a bit rough, and seem rather interested in me. You may think this sounds absurd, but, you know, I have been in Algeria, and, well, I gather what I wrote was none too popular.'

'I see,' said the voice at the other end. 'Just wait a minute, will you?'

There was a pause. Then he came back on the line.

'Now, where exactly are you?' I told him. 'Look,' he said, 'if you're a bit uneasy, we'll ask the police in the area, someone in uniform, to come down and get you out.'

At this moment I saw out of the corner of my eye the five men disappearing rapidly up the steps from the basement.

'Look,' I said. 'After Algeria I'm not even too keen on the French police. And, incidentally, we're profiling Lacoste this week, and he knows.'

'Oh, I don't think it's *that*,' said the man at the Embassy. 'Oh no. Not that.'

'No? Well, maybe not. But I can believe anything here nowadays.'

Feeling by now slightly ridiculous, I went upstairs from the basement and sat down once more at the bar, where I ordered a brandy. No one came. I ordered another brandy. The Dauphine was still deserted. After about a quarter of an hour a pleasant-looking girl with a silk headscarf came in. She looked round, standing in the doorway, then came up to me. I wondered at first if she was a very proper-looking tart; but this didn't seem likely. It happened quickly.

'Oh, Monsieur,' she said to me, 'is there a second exit?'

Then, without another word, she walked round to the other side of the bar and disappeared through a door at the back, somewhere near the kitchen. I watched the girl go, and sat, feeling puzzled. I sat like this for about five minutes. Then it occurred to me: 'Second exit,' she had said; and she had used it. Was she tipping me off? She must have been. No policeman was coming in to escort me out. The girl had been it. Was she a policewoman; or what? Anyhow, I paid for my brandy and the earlier coffee, and walked round the bar and out of the back door taken by the girl.

It was a November night, rainy, with lights reflected in the puddles. A taxi drew up in front of me. Had I waved it down? In retrospect, it almost seems that I had not. I climbed in, and the driver moved off.

'The British Embassy, please,' I told him.

It almost seemed he knew where we were going beforehand. We crossed the gleam of the Seine and eventually turned into the rue du Faubourg St Honoré. We drove straight through the gates and halted by the steps to the entrance hall. I went up in the lift to the office of the man I had telephoned.

'Hullo,' he said.

We shook hands.

'Well,' I said. 'Thanks. No policeman came to fetch me. But a girl in a silk scarf showed me a second exit.'

If the man at the Embassy was surprised by what I said, he didn't show it then, though the business of the girl had surprised me.

'If I'm feeling windy, I always believe in giving a scream,' I said.

'Well, you know,' he said, 'in situations like this I think perhaps they may sometimes harass journalists who are being a bit difficult; make life difficult for *them*. Was there a riot, stone-throwing, anything like that?'

I said that there wasn't.

'You know,' he said, 'you ought to go and hear one of Jacques Soustelle's political meetings. He really does say some things.'

I said I'd try to. Soustelle I didn't like.

The man at the Embassy asked me if I would go and see the man at the Quai d'Orsay who had translated my Algerian series for French official perusal. I said I would, and he arranged it then on the telephone.

'He's a nice man,' said the man at the Embassy. 'Used to be French Consul in Cardiff, I think.'

The next morning I went round to the Quai d'Orsay and met this official. He was small, round, and dark, in a dark office.

'We were interested in your series,' he said a little coldly. 'The only thing we couldn't forgive was your insulting the honour of the French Army. That was too much.'

'Oh?' I said.

I told him I thought General Massu a fool or a criminal. And, perhaps unwisely, I mentioned the names of some very rich men who must share much of the blame for what was happening in Algeria.

The interview did not last long.

As the official was showing me out into the passage, he mentioned Claude Bourdet, then editor of the left-wing *France Observateur*.

'You know, he's collecting funds for the FLN,' said the official.

'If that's true,' I said, 'why don't you arrest him?'

Paris then seemed full of people, often those in authority, who would blacken anyone if it suited them. Did it reflect the state of France? Or did the same thing happen in London?

After leaving the Quai d'Orsay, I noticed I was being followed. Imagination could play tricks, and I knew my nerves were none too good, drink, lack of sleep and black coffee contributing. But I *was* being followed: he was a youngish man with upstanding brown hair, a pale face, and a fawn raincoat, his right hand in his pocket. I was sure of it; and I didn't like it.

I decided to visit again a Swedish journalist called Vinde,

who a day or two before had given me revealing material for the Lacoste profile. Vinde was a solid, cultivated, silver-haired man, who was later to become editor of a Stockholm paper. He had already told me all he knew about Lacoste, which was a great deal, and some of it curious. He said he and his wife had recently visited Algiers, and they had taken with them the series I had written on the Algerian war in the *Observer*.

'It was written *avec flamme*,' Vinde had told me. 'But after spending a short time in Algeria I was convinced you were right.'

I had thanked him.

Now, thinking myself followed, I set out again for Vinde's apartment, on foot. The young man in the raincoat was still behind. Vinde lived not far from the Invalides, and I crossed cold open spaces. I went straight up in the lift to Vinde's apartment. When I left the lift, someone rang for it, and the lift descended. Standing in the gloom before the door, I rang the bell of the apartment: I heard it echoing inside; no one came to the door. I rang several times. The lift was coming up again. It stopped behind me, on the floor I was on. I gave Vinde's bell a last ring. Then I turned round. I saw in the stationary lift, through the criss-crossed metal of the cage, the young man whom I had suspected was following me. He was younger than I had thought, and his face was very pale. I looked at him, and he looked at me. The light was dim; no one was about. He still had his right hand in the pocket of his raincoat. He made no attempt to open the door of the lift. We looked at each other, saying nothing. Then the young man pressed the button of the lift and descended. I remained standing there. I gave Vinde's bell one more ring and waited. Then, without calling the lift, I walked down the spiral stone stairs to the street.

At about this moment the paper decided they didn't yet want to profile Lacoste after all.

'Write more about the situation in Paris,' they said to me on the telephone.

The girl secretary in our Paris office thought I was behaving oddly; so did the assistant correspondent in Paris at that time.

'I saw you near the Invalides,' he said. 'You weren't being followed.'

I disagreed. Yet I was drinking too much. I had begun to have an odd, fuzzy feeling in my feet. One morning I had an idea the secretary must have put something in my coffee: something to calm me down, was it? Was this what was making my feet fuzzy? Yes, that was it. She must have given me a pill.

With these suspicions in my mind, I walked out of the Paris office and set off fast for the British Embassy.

'They're drugging me,' I thought.

Was I suffering from delusions, or were these things really happening to me?

I was feeling distinctly odd: everything seemed heightened, clear; the light seemed a strange blue that November day, and yet the blue had a pink and sometimes even an orange edge, like the edge of a rainbow. Still walking fast, I crossed the Champ de Mars below the Eiffel Tower.

'This,' I thought, 'was where my lucky handkerchief landed ten years ago, when I flew it from the top up there.'

My feet were still fuzzy. The light was still strange. I walked faster still, swinging my arms hard.

'Swinging your arms like that is a sign of madness,' that adjutant had once told me years before in the Army.

Beneath the Eiffel Tower was a man with a dark blue hat, a dark blue coat, and a dark blue chin to his thin dark face. On a strap round his neck he carried a tray of small lead models of the Eiffel Tower. Suddenly it seemed very important to buy one of these lead models, as proof. As proof of what? As proof of reality and evil: as proof that these strange things were happening to me. I bought a model Eiffel Tower with a dark blue rosette attached to it, and walked on fast, holding it tightly in my hand. I crossed the Seine and at last reached the British Embassy. I hurried up to the office of the man who had helped me before.

'They're drugging me,' I said. 'The girl at our office put something in my coffee.'

The man at the Embassy took this well; but he gave me a look.

'Israel may be in it, too,' I said. 'The French have persuaded Israel that if Algeria wins independence, Nasser will use the

Algerian Army, the best in the Arab world, against the State of Israel. But this isn't true.'

I paused, then blurted out: 'You're a Catholic, aren't you?'

'Yee-rss,' he said, recoiling slightly.

'Look,' I said. 'Do you know just how bad Algeria is?'

'I think so,' he said. 'Yes.'

'Well,' I said, 'I'll tell you something. I was on television not so long ago with a Catholic priest. I told him I couldn't believe in original sin. Now, after Algeria, I can. People didn't believe what was happening in Nazi Germany before the war. Now the same sort of thing is happening in Algeria. So look out. Look out. I'm warning you of the evil in Algeria.'

'I think you ought to take a bit of a rest,' said the man at the Embassy. 'Try and forget Algeria for a bit.' He paused, then remarked, 'Look. I really must do the bag. Forgive me, will you?'

'O.K.,' I said. 'I'm sorry.'

When I went down in the Embassy lift the old grey-haired porter operating it was friendly.

Back in the Paris office I rang up the paper in London.

'Look,' I said. 'I don't think I'm too well. I think maybe I ought to come home.'

I caught a plane that evening. From London Airport I took a taxi to the editor's London house. When I arrived several people were having dinner there.

'Funny things happened in Paris,' I said. I told them some of the things. 'Do I seem a bit odd?' I asked.

'No,' said the editor's wife. Perhaps she was being polite.

After dinner the editor drove me deep into what was either Kilburn or West Hampstead to see a doctor. The doctor was a thin dark man.

'I think you need a good night's sleep,' he said, after I had told him of some of the things that seemed to have been happening to me in Paris. 'Here's a pill,' he added. 'Take it when you go to bed tonight.'

The editor drove me home to Jill. It was good of him. That night I slept well without taking the pill.

'Fine,' said the editor on the telephone next morning, a Saturday, when I told him I was in good form and wanted to write about Paris. 'Go ahead and write.'

I went into the office and started to write the piece: 'Strange things are happening in Paris. Officials will say . . .'

I took a sip from a cup of coffee. Then I left the room for a moment. I came back. A colleague was sitting at the desk opposite mine. He was a great friend, originally from Hungary. The only thing I had against him at that period was that he sometimes seemed too right-wing. And I suspected that he was against the Arab world in general, feeling it threatened Israel. I didn't want Israel threatened, either; but at least the Algerians were unlikely to do this, it seemed to me.

I sat down at my desk, and looked again at the piece I had started: 'Strange things are happening in Paris. Officials will say . . .' That didn't seem good. I decided to start again, and screwed up the paper into a ball. I took another gulp of coffee, stood up, and stretched. Suddenly I felt it: my feet were becoming fuzzy again, that strange feeling. I looked down at my coffee, and then across at my colleague. Had he also tampered with my coffee, as I thought the girl secretary had done in Paris? It felt like it. Was it a plot? I said nothing. I left the room and went down to the editor's office. I burst in.

'Look,' I said to the editor. 'Someone's put something in my coffee. I know who's done it: it's . . .'

'You can't mean that seriously,' said the editor. 'You ought to go home and take it easy for the rest of the week-end. Whether or not some of the things you think happened to you in Paris did or did not happen, it must have been a nightmare. Go home and take it easy.'

'All right,' I said. 'All right. I will.'

I went home, and I never wrote that piece on Paris and the strange things that were happening there. I gave the small lead model of the Eiffel Tower to my son, James.

England seemed safe. Its demonstrations were without violence. The most important job I had in the next few months was the covering of the Campaign for Nuclear Disarmament's first Easter March to the Atomic Weapons Research Establishment at Aldermaston. Whatever the later vicissitudes of CND, the first march was a great thing.

We went down the Bath Road to London Airport in the rain under the dripping skeletons of trees. Viscounts went up, booming and whining in the mist, and snow and slush lay heavy on the verges. In the grey, pervading wet, the column stretched for nearly a mile: a forest of emblems on short handles bobbed in the haze: the *motif* like a long-finned rocket with a circle: the semaphore of N D for nuclear disarmament.

A girl in jeans, soaked, plodded under a great banner, 'Save the World'. Snow still clung to the plough and the sad turnip fields. A scratch band played 'It takes a Worried Man to Sing a Worried Song', and the notes of the clarinet floated clearly. A foreman from the B O A C maintenance staff joined the marchers, and this brought a ragged cheer.

'I'm glad it's raining,' someone said.

The Rev. Donald Soper, wearing a plastic raincoat, a plastic fore-and-aft cap, a leather dispatch rider's jacket and, then, his black robes, was up at the head; on his right was a spruce-bearded figure with grey hair, cap, and a fur-lined jacket. Miss Pat Arrowsmith, organizing secretary of the march, was in the leading three: she was astonishingly young, with black hair, a bright face, a pack on her back, a pale mauve raincoat and red luminous socks. There were students in a variety of raincoats; the old and the young. There was a ginger-bearded man in great tall boots and a wide-brimmed canvas hat who looked like a Canadian trapper: he'd once caught snakes in South America, and he believed in brotherhood.

There was a young girl among those carrying the large banner of the Twickenham branch of CND (a painted group of father in dark suit, mother in blue, and small child in yellow in her arms), and she had very pink legs below her green jeans, and she seemed very young.

We stopped for lunch at an inn within sight of London Airport. Wet, angular figures shambled about; steam rose off damp clothes; the clarinet tootled an old folk-song. It felt almost medieval. Religious pacifists; socialists of no particular party allegiance; one or two Communists; a Tory who supported Suez;

a lot of girls with long hair and earnest expressions; a great raw-boned Irishman in a cap who said, 'Those who are not here are the mad ones.'

It could have been easy to mock them. Someone sensing this said, 'What is it, "Blessed are the peacemakers"?' He asked Dr Soper about the sermon on the Mount. 'What was it, "Blessed are the meek . . ."?'

' "For they shall inherit the earth," ' said Dr Soper, 'and that's what Mark Twain said at Queen Victoria's Diamond Jubilee. But it's a lot more true of a lot of people walking in the rain.'

There were many cars and vans with posters following the march. One was an elderly black-and-silver Rolls-Royce: it halted, its windscreen wipers still working, and three tiny rosy-cheeked girls in blue, left by themselves, gazed from it towards the mournful fields.

The band started up again with 'Basin Street', and the marchers formed up for the next leg to Slough. A radio van was interviewing some of the marchers against a wall of the pub.

'What can they say when they're trapped like that by reporters?' someone said. 'Why are they here? It's a crusade if you like. They're doing something. They're doing something about this feeling of helplessness.'

I could not get Algeria out of my mind.

In Paris, the FLN failed to assassinate Jacques Soustelle, who had been Minister in Algiers before Lacoste, and whom I now regarded as the man chiefly responsible for the evils in Algeria. Soustelle had investigated and written about the Aztec civilization, and I persuaded myself that an Aztec charm had saved his life.

Every time I drove from our house in the suburb to Fleet Street, it seemed to me that the same large Austin Westminster, fawn with a pink stripe, followed me through the mist, its orange fog lamp vibrating and glinting in my mirror. I was getting a persecution complex. I mentioned the Austin and its blazing fog lamp to a woman I knew.

'They're following me,' I said. 'They think after what I've been writing, particularly on Algeria, that I'm a Communist.'

She didn't know I was already a bit crazy.

'Well,' she said, 'I worked for MI5 during the war. And we did things to people: followed them like that. Exactly the same.'

'Oh?' I said.

'Thank goodness Patrick [her husband] in his journalism hasn't got mixed up in any situation like this,' she added.

The putsch came in Algeria. Soustelle, smuggled out of Paris in the boot of a car, arrived in Algiers and behaved for a time like a dictator, loving the acclaim of the hysterical crowds. De Gaulle came back, Soustelle was ousted.

I flew to Tunis to report the situation there. I interviewed Bourguiba and kept in touch with the leaders of the FLN and of the FLN army operating from Tunisian soil.

One night I went to a seedy open-air night-club just outside Tunis. I asked a cool but attractive French blonde to dance. She had just done a cabaret turn, singing in a mellow, fluting voice, wearing black tights on her long legs. As we danced under the stars, I told her I was a journalist, not long back from Algiers. She remained cool, and unimpressed. Suddenly she said: 'You know that I'm a man?'

'*Oui, bien sûr,*' I replied, without thinking.

Then I realized what she had said. I broke away from her in mid-dance, leaving her by herself on the floor. I went to the bar, and asked for a drink.

'That blonde says she's a man,' I told the barman.

'All the girls in the troupe are men,' he said. 'Didn't you know?'

The war in Algeria continued.

Back in London, the *Universities and Left Review* asked me to speak on The Algerian War in St Pancras Town Hall.

'Even if you're abroad, we'll fly you back specially for the meeting,' said the voice on the telephone. 'We'll pay all your expenses.'

'Well,' I thought, 'anything to tell people what's going on in Algeria. They ought to know.'

My family and I went on holiday to Cornwall. I was writing a Profile of the FLN leaders. On a Monday I took the train from Penzance to London for the meeting in St Pancras Town Hall.

My youngest brother, Andy, met me in London, and we had a drink in a pub.

'Have you prepared what you're going to say?' he asked.

'No,' I said. 'I'll just tell them one or two stories of what I saw in Algeria.'

'Well,' he said doubtfully. 'I suppose you know what you're doing.'

The meeting on Algeria and the names of the speakers had been heavily advertised in the *New Statesman* and elsewhere.

We reached St Pancras Town Hall, and I fought my way into a side room, where Claude Bourdet, editor of *France-Observateur*, was lecturing some people, before the real meeting began, on how Socialists ought to end the war in Algeria. This somehow put my back up. Plenty of French Socialists, including Guy Mollet and Robert Lacoste, had had their chance of ending the Algerian war, by then four years old, and they hadn't achieved much. I walked out of the side room and bumped into Dick Clements, editor of *Tribune*, and I told him this.

'I hope you're not going to say that here,' Dick said. 'You know, this audience won't like it.'

'Well look, Dick,' I said, 'so-called Socialists like Mollet and Lacoste have had their chance of ending the Algerian war. Now let's see what de Gaulle can do. I may vote Labour in England, but I'm not going to make propaganda for French Socialism just for the sake of appearances.'

Dick shook his head: 'People here tonight won't like it.'

Well, they didn't, very much, because after I'd been on my feet a minute or two someone passed me a note saying, 'Two minutes more.' The note put me right off my stroke. I was trying to tell the audience what the war in Algeria was really like: how they put young prisoners in a truck and paraded them round Tebessa to the strains of 'Madelon', and how, afterwards, a padre ordered champagne; how men and girls were tortured. But somehow I never finished what I wanted to say.

'I believe the German occupation of France has had a big effect on the war in Algeria,' I said. 'Because suffering, except in rare instances, never improves people, but causes further suffering. It degrades us all.'

A black man jumped up and said: 'How do you explain Kenya?'

'All right,' I said. 'I wasn't there.'

I sat down, knowing that my first and last attempt at speech-making had been a heavy flop.

I didn't ask for my expenses.

When Andy and I left St Pancras Town Hall, it was a lovely summer evening, and a man was playing a barrel-organ. I took the night train back to Cornwall.

On the cool floor of the larder of our holiday bungalow in Cornwall was a five-foot conger eel: it was coiled so that the jaws nearly closed on the tail, and one eye, where it had been hooked, was white and blind.

The conger had a bitter, oily smell. Its head was like a bull terrier's. Some people said they barked, though I had never heard one.

This was one of the best we had caught. When Andy had hauled it thrashing out of the water the night before, a young stonemason with a red beard had hit it with the tiller bar: with each blow the conger had gasped. Even then it had locked its tail round the small boat's propeller shaft. The stonemason had got it free at last, and had flung it among its brothers in a large wicker basket, where it had writhed and glistened in the light of the pressure lamp.

We had been anchored, fishing just off the bottom at fifteen fathoms, and I had got one up thirty feet when he had broken the tarred line and gone off with a four-pound lead.

'He must have been seventy or eighty pound to break that line,' the stonemason had said.

I had got into another that I could not shift, and he nearly took me overboard before straightening the six-inch hook and getting away. Perhaps his tail had been round a rock. It was sport all right; but in those congers was a will to live that made me feel guilty. At least we would eat our big one.

'I don't fancy they congers, somehow,' the stonemason had said. 'Snakes and that.'

We had flung ours into the Ford van and gone home at one in

175

the morning. And now the conger was on the larder floor: perhaps he was a snake, but he was washed by the sea, and beautiful. In a corner near by a crayfish was creaking intermittently in a damp sack.

We sharpened a carving knife on the stone steps and took the conger down to the beach. Andy gutted him on the edge of the breakers.

'Oh!' said my daughter Joanna. 'Look at all that.'

She considered for a moment, uncertain what she felt. Then she decided: 'It's the most wonderful thing in the world.'

In the conger's stomach were several gleaming slices of mackerel, showing he had been busy with our baits before we had got him.

The crayfish was for lunch, and he was so big that we had to boil the water in the bread bin. I put him in head first, a moment I could not watch. He was ready in thirty minutes, pink and steaming: a giant prawn of seven pounds.

The carapace of the tail came off with one jerk, and there was a marvellous curve of resilient flesh; the head split with a stroke of the knife; the thin shell of the legs cracked in the hand, and you drew out those miraculous slivers. Everyone stood round the table, holding their breath.

'You know,' said James afterwards, 'we shouldn't have eaten him. He was too interesting. We ought to have somehow dried him and kept him on the mantelpiece.'

'He's done what he was made for,' said Joanna.

She was keeping butterfish in an aquarium, a white salad bowl, and now and again blew bubbles in the water with the outside casing of a Biro, to aerate them. The butterfish crouched beneath seaweed and a stone: they had been dark in the rock pool, but now, like chameleons, they were a light colour in the white bowl.

That afternoon we lay in the sun in a sandy hollow surrounded by coarse sea-grass, and felt well. Above were red notice boards warning of dangerous bathing. Far off, the brown Lizard ran out into a cold blue sea.

'Listen,' said Andy. 'See that ship right out there? You can hear its engines. Astonishing.'

There was a faint thumping. But in the end the thumping

turned out to be the strange, underwaterish rhythm of 'Tie Me Kangaroo Down, Sport', coming from a small transistor radio belonging to a fed-up-looking North Countryman with a big family and sand in his turn-ups. He was sitting near by, yearning for his mates.

Joanna decided to release her butterfish. She carried them down and tipped them out of the salad bowl on to the wet sand rippled by the incoming tide. They turned towards the waves and raised their heads, scenting freedom. Soon they were gone.

Walking up for tea, she said: 'Animals like being eaten. It's their job. They don't know their heads are going to be cut off. But what about people in the olden days? Didn't they know, either? Or were they a bit trembly?'

We returned to London. For months afterwards in our suburb there was a ghostly trace of the conger, grey yet unmistakable, on the dark floorboards of our Ford van, where he had lain on that night he was caught.

Part Five

I never wrote about Algeria again. But I tried to go there once more, not on the paper's account. I wished to take time off from journalism, and travel across Algeria with the rebels, from the Tunisian border to Morocco. My aim was to write a book about it; and a firm of publishers gave me a handsome advance. I intended going with Herb, an American friend, who had a black beard and shaved his head. When my father, then a sick man, heard we were going, he gave me a cigar as a present for Herb. But at the last moment the paper would not agree to my taking time off, feeling that it might be an embarrassment if I were involved in any troubles on the rebel side in Algeria. Instead, they sent me to Formosa, to write about the American Seventh Fleet, the greatest in the world, then steaming within striking distance of China.

The offshore island of Quemoy was under Communist shell-fire when I visited it. A village on the island opposite the Chinese mainland was badly damaged. Civilians began to appear, men in blue shorts, women in Chinese trousers or black shiny split skirts, their fine black hair combed back in a bun. The men and women were beautifully made, their calves strong and ankles slim. They were oyster fishers, but had no oyster harvest nowadays. A boy carried his tiny brother in a sling on his back; the baby had a broad, interested face. Two small girls were losing their front teeth.

Clean-looking pigs were in pens made – like the whole village – of granite blocks. Ducks swam on a pale green pond lined with short willows.

As we were leaving we discovered the village shelter revetted with bags of clinking oyster shells. There were a lot of people deep in a gloomy tunnel, apparently all men. Was the resigned acceptance of these people a good or a dangerous thing?

On returning to Formosa from Quemoy, I found that there was a US Navy aircraft waiting to take me immediately to the Seventh Fleet. After about an hour's flying the pilot said: 'You can see them up eight miles ahead.'

There they were through the aircraft's windscreen: a destroyer, a heavy cruiser, and the great aircraft carrier USS *Midway*, silver-grey trailing white on a blue sea. Ships that could change the world.

We circled over the carrier and watched swept-wing bombers slide off her flight-deck like toys. Then it was our turn: the undercarriage grumbled down, the note of the engines rose as the propellers went into fine pitch, and we slid in over the *Midway*'s wake. Suddenly full power came on again, we climbed and turned and the carrier's island superstructure sidled by at an angle: a wave-off. Next time we touched and a great hand held us as the arrestor cables grabbed our tail-hook.

We climbed out on to steel six inches thick surfaced with rubber compound and in the harsh sunlight young men in ear-phoned helmets, red, blue, brown, green, and yellow jerseys and oil-stained non-slip suède shoes said 'Hey!' and 'Wow!' and it felt like an American football team. There were several Negroes among them and they all carried jacks and spanners and clasp knives at their belts. A Texan lieutenant with a thin face, wearing pale khaki, got my name right first time and said: 'It's a very great pleasure to meet you, sir.' A horn gargled in the paraffin-scented wind and a jet fighter with a raked tail vanished below on a lift. Then the ship's chaplain welcomed me aboard by name over the public address system. We might have been on land except for the just perceptible beat of engines far below. We were at the heart of the most powerful fleet ever.

'Nuclear' was a word you seldom heard. 'Special weapons' was the most you usually got. Wandering far down among the *Midway*'s bulkheads you might see in red letters on a metal door:

Restricted Area
Special Weapons Center

It was hard to realize what was behind that door.

Up above, loaded Skywarriors weighing seventy thousand pounds were getting the 'catshot', being steam-catapulted off the angled flight-deck. You could hear the engines on full power, and then the thump of the catapult reverberated through the great ship. Each aircraft, like a flying dogfish, edged up whining to the catapults, and its wings and tail unfolded into position. Steam escaped from the catapult tracks, and the catapult operators attached the bridle to the shuttle and hooked up on to the aircraft. When the aircraft was in position, a metal ramp rose vertically from the deck behind the jet-pipe of each engine to protect the following aircraft from the blast. The *Midway* steamed fast into the wind, and the catapult officer in yellow shirt and helmet stood in the centre of the deck and gave the pilot the 'turn-up' wave: the pilot opened up his engines and saluted, with the transparent hatch of his canopy open lest he and his crew had to get out in a hurry; watchers' ears were hurt by the cry of the turbines and their faces scorched by burning paraffin; the catapult officer crouched, pointed once down the deck, twice – and the Skywarrior was away, disappearing into low cloud with a faint trail of smoke.

On the walls of the air-conditioned ready-room far below were pictures and instructions to men taken prisoner. At the end were these words: 'I will never forget that I am an American fighting man, responsible for my actions, and dedicated to the principles which made my country free. I will trust in my God and in the United States of America.'

Much later all but the watches slept: pilots of twenty-two; pilots nearing middle age, with coloured photographs of their crew-cut children standing beside the electric razors in their berths; in all, in this ship, 3,600 officers and men in a hive of bulkheads smelling of paint and warm rubber. And you thought of the *Midway*'s miles of plastic piping for spraying contamination.

The public address system was still on quietly and a male choir sang, just audibly, to the whole ship 'Don't Fence Me In', 'Home on the Range' and a song whose only words seemed to be 'Far, Far Away, Far, Far Away'.

On my last day in Formosa a heavy, elderly American journalist, who wore thick-lensed glasses, said to me: 'You know, John, I think we ought to go now, go, go, go with the Seventh Fleet: put Peking in the ash-can.'

A few weeks later I visited America. The State Department had invited me as a result of what I had written on Algeria. Jill and the children came to see me off at London Airport, where we were ushered by mistake into a VIP's lounge: the children, in identical blue overcoats with velvet collars, sat in a row on the window-sill eating cocktail biscuits and gazing out like small birds at the great fishlike aircraft gleaming in the winter night.

After Algeria and the Far East, I was in an odd state on the American visit, and I took refuge in drink, wild talk and night-clubs.

Once we were taken round a supermarket on the outskirts of Washington. I bought a great, red, clinking Alaska crab, broke its legs like sticks, and handed it round to the NATO journalists who made up our party. The crab may have done some good: even a Greek journalist in an Athenian stetson seemed to un-bend, though he did not want to make friends with Englishmen at that time, since Cyprus was at its bloodiest and we were still in occupation. In our hotel that night the Greek was, despite Cyprus, friendly, and he agreed to come to the bar, where he took off his stetson, revealing the baldest head I had ever seen: it shone like a white sun, and from it rose the scent of polish. I was so sur-prised and even embarrassed that I looked at his feet, and con-gratulated him on his suède shoes, which were of a dark and unusual brown.

'You like these shoes?' he said. 'I will have a pair made and send you from Greece when I return.'

I thanked him very much.

By the time we reached El Paso, in Texas, I was seeing every-thing in a pink, taut light, and my brain was whirling like a set of blades. On our first night in El Paso we went over the border to Juarez, in Mexico, and I gulped tequila in a strange bar. My perception seemed heightened. We returned to El Paso on a tram, and an Italian journalist and I took a tour round the town on foot. We found houses that were just façades, made of wood, paint, and plaster, as though for a film set.

One of our hosts in El Paso was a millionaire with a broad pig face and glasses, who drove a huge car. He scorned the Mexicans. One day he took us into the poorest quarter of Juarez to show how it compared with the American way of life. He said illegal Mexican immigrants tried to get across the border into Texas, and implied that harsh things were done to them if they were caught. We returned across the Texan border, and he took us to an appalling circular drive-in café, where we filled up with petrol and ate our meal without leaving the car. Visions of a future legless race winked at me.

One morning, early, we were made honorary citizens of Juarez (or was it El Paso?), wore clanking badges, and had breakfast with the Mayor and an extraordinary British journalist who said he had come from Canada. This man had long hair, straggly moustache, a grey face, glasses, and deformed hands with which he whirled his knife and fork as though he were a circus performer. I wondered if he was a lackey of the State Department, sent to unbalance me.

That day we saw the American Army let off rockets from the desert into an ice-blue sky. In the afternoon we returned to our hotel, where we rested. I had the impression that they had in some way changed my room, or put me in another. For the room now seemed only three-quarters as large as it had been before, and it felt as though the walls were closing in on me. Everything was the same, but smaller. I had with my washing things a piece of soap that I had picked up from the basin the day before and not used. It was still in its paper, and I compared it with a new piece of soap in the basin: the soap of the day before was about a quarter larger than the piece of soap in the basin on this afternoon. Otherwise both were identical: 'Hotel Cortez, El Paso', was written on the paper of both pieces of soap; and, above a tiny map of the U.S.A., were the words: 'Affiliated National Hotels. Host to the Nation'. On the side it said: 'Cashmere bouquet'. Were things being done to me?

We flew to Los Angeles. On a visit to Hollywood, while we were sitting in an enormous, almost fleshy, office that seemed to have a life of its own, I made a scene: I shouted at a long-suffering man, a film tycoon of second degree, and asked him what good films Hollywood could claim to have made lately. He reeled off a long list in reply, and this made me laugh very loudly.

We had lunch, which tasted as though it had been pre-digested, in a huge canteen. Cary Grant was in there eating, so they said. The producer who was our host, a small, sad Jew, said how worried he was by the smog over Los Angeles. He spoke as though it were a living emanation, a sinister portent, a cloud with a brain, come to suppress and finally suffocate the city.

'We don't know what to do about it. We don't know what the cause is.'

The roads of Los Angeles were wide and double-tracked and disappeared like silvery ribbons into the distance; gliding along them you knew the world was round, and you felt you might fall off into space. You wanted good brakes on your car.

Our State Department guide, a Levantine with very blue eyes, took us to some well-known place in Hollywood where there were the footprints of famous stars in the concrete. Almost all those that had left footprints were now dead. It was a threatening place, and seemed a reminder that nothing kills like success. Had they been people out of their depth? That evening I shouted at people for staring at me outside the lifts in the hotel. The hotel was cavernous, the decorations were in yellow plastic, and there seemed a reek of mammon. Few clocks appeared to agree about the time.

The next morning, finding my right shoe was in trouble, the sole coming apart from the upper, I sought a cobbler. I was told where I could find one, and on the way passed through a large grey square which, in the strange, silvery light of that day, was filled with bums, some of them making speeches, with dusty pigeons sitting on their arms, heads and shoulders. When I reached the cobbler, he turned out to be an elderly Negro wearing glasses.

'You've come just in time,' he said, examining the shoe.

His words made me believe that I was a Messiah, come just in time to save America. While the Negro mended my shoe, I sat, with a feeling of responsibility, elation, and yet, also, of calm.

We next visited the Lockheed Aircraft factory, and saw the Electra production lines. This aircraft was in many ways like an enlarged Viscount; but not quite. They say that if an aircraft looks right, it is right. To me, there was something a little displeasing about the Electra: was it slightly hump-backed, even lumpish? I mentioned that the aircraft didn't look quite right to me to the company employee showing us round, and he laughed, humouring me. We saw one of the first production Electras take off, and, as I stood with our group, it was noticeable that the other journalists shunned me; they were embarrassed. I walked out on to the runway and watched the Electra take off over my head into the sun, its broad propellers purring. That very aircraft was soon to crash into the East River, New York, killing, among others, a client of the architect Mies van der Rohe, then the employer of my brother Adrian. It put Adrian out of a job.

We went on that morning to Disneyland, where, after lunch with a delightful uniformed hostess, we boarded an old-time Mississippi river boat on the lake in Disneyland's ornamental park. There was no traditional Negro jazz band on board, and I asked for one: they provided it.

Back in our hotel, I began to think that the younger conducting officer of our group, a slender, high-pitched young man in thick dark-rimmed glasses, was inserting microphones – or even apparatus to pick up my thoughts – behind the bed and radiators in my room. That evening the older conducting officer, the Levantine, took us to a strange bar and restaurant with glass walls on rocky ground high above Los Angeles. I thought the people in this place were in reality actors and actresses playing the part of students, and that in some way this was a phoney world laid on for me.

'Come on,' I said to the Levantine. 'I'm a journalist, not a bloody tourist.'

The Levantine was not pleased, but the wise Italian journalist in our group smoothed things over.

That night I turned up the radio in my room – it was on the whole time, and all you had to do was turn up the volume – to listen to a news bulletin. 'Ninety-four children were today burnt to death in a school in Chicago,' said the announcer in a harsh voice. All the news bulletins I heard in America in those days seemed to be about death and violence, and the voices of the announcers relished the theme.

Before I went to sleep I rang up my brother Adrian in Chicago, and told him my view of Los Angeles: 'It's a dead city.'

The next morning I went out to post a parcel to my son, James, in England: the parcel contained a small ornamental toy pistol and a Mexican dagger. Walking to the post office, below the massive buildings, and not gliding in a car, I felt exposed, as though stripped of a skin. I was directed to the post office through a great garage, where large cars seemed to be rolling backwards slowly, by themselves, and the only attendant was a thin man with dull eyes and a face like clay. The post office was below the garage; a Negro was in there. As I was filling in a form for the parcel, I began to sing a hymn.

On our last night in Los Angeles, a German journalist and I went to a night-club, heard the music of the cool Negro Buddy Collette, which struck me as a mixture of Bach and Louis Armstrong, and went to bed too late after too much whisky and ginger ale.

We went to the station early next morning. The station reminded me of a great, green, satanic temple. It seemed a bad place to bring children, and I felt a great weight upon mind and body. There was some time to wait for our train to San Francisco. To counter the effects of no sleep and too much drink, I went to the station's cafeteria and drank black coffee after black coffee. I felt as though in a trance, and had an incipient headache. A small, fair girl, standing with her mother and grandfather, looked at me with what I thought was adoration, and the feeling that I was a Messiah again overwhelmed me.

'I had too much to drink last night,' I said to the grandfather, who was wearing an old-timer's hat.

'I never touch it, brother,' he told me.

He belonged to some sect.

I finished my last black coffee, left the cafeteria, passed through a maze of railings and by a man in a green uniform who punched my ticket and shouted at me, out on to a platform long and white, longer than I could have imagined. The train to San Francisco had gone, taking with it the rest of the group. I was alone.

I had left my typewriter and a suitcase containing my passport unattended on the ground in the middle of the central hall of Los Angeles station; I wanted to be rid of them. Eventually a man took them and deposited them at the left-luggage counter. Without possessions, I took a bus to Santa Barbara; we rolled along a silver, double-track highway. At Santa Barbara I took a silver train to San Francisco. It was comfortable. I drank from an iced-water fountain at the end of the compartment: afterwards I noticed an elderly woman with blue hair and strange, whorled glasses go up and use the same cardboard cup I had drunk from. The train slid through vast fields with leaden furrows stretching into the distance. Then we passed through a wasteland full of oil wells: dark shapes like prehistoric birds pecking and drinking from the earth, using up its goodness. There was not a human being in sight. There was a mist over the land, and the light, though silvery, was dark, for the sun could not get through.

It was night when we reached San Francisco. I took a taxi to the address at which my brother Adrian had once lived. We seemed to go up and down lighted hills as we passed through the town. A Volkswagen was ahead, and I believed it was guiding us. At last we stopped at an apartment house. I climbed the stairs towards the sound of a girl's voice singing in Russian to a balalaika. The door of the apartment was open, and a party was in progress. I explained who I was, and the people there were kind. It was a Saturday night, and I decided that I ought neither to eat nor to drink till midnight. I lay down in a passage and took cat naps, interspersed with yogic exercises. No one seemed surprised. When midnight struck, I got to my feet, drank, and ate red caviare. Then I decided I should ring up Jill in London. A handsome girl showed me to her room, where there was a red telephone. I asked for the number. As I was waiting, I had a vision: there was a faint snap, and there beside me on a small table, which had been bare immediately before, stood a large glass of drink and a burning cigarette; there was another snap, and drink and cigarette vanished. Then Jill came through clearly on the line. I had woken her up early in the morning.

'You sound as though you have second sight,' she said.

I was speaking in a slow, drugged way. We talked for about half an hour.

'For God's sake return our television set,' I said. 'We don't want television.'

I was horrified by the television I had seen in America.

Afterwards the girl operator told me the cost of the call: one hundred and thirty dollars. I found that I had in my wallet exactly this sum: one hundred and ten dollars, and the rest in English money. I gave it all to the handsome girl from whose room I had telephoned. Now I had got rid not only of my passport but of all my money. I felt free.

I rejoined the party. In one room a silver-haired man with a Central European accent seemed to be holding court, with people sitting at his feet. I chose the other room, which was noisier and more anarchic. I sat on a pouf and gave a blond ex-boxer advice about his marriage. I told a woman psychiatrist my view of the space-race: 'They're trying to prove they're men. People should stay on the ground.' She nodded earnestly. I was a terrible bore.

I slept that night on the kitchen floor of the apartment, though the handsome girl, owner of the red telephone, had offered me a bed. The next morning, a Sunday, another occupant of the apartment, which seemed to be very large, made me a cup of coffee and demonstrated his radio, which he had built himself. He was a slight man called Charlie, and a friend of my brother Adrian. Charlie showed me that it was easy to get trash on his radio, but difficult to get good music, which was a question of fine tuning. This struck me as sinister.

I said good-bye to Charlie, and left. Charlie, who knew I had no money, had advised me to go to the offices of some British organization. But, since it was a Sunday, the offices were shut. As I was standing in the street in the sun and stroking my chin, I got into conversation with a red-haired girl. She said that like almost everyone in America she was taking Dexadrin to slim. She said that her husband, a Negro, was in prison, framed by the police. She offered to show me round San Francisco, and did.

As we were walking up one street we spotted a Union Jack, and went in through the door. Inside there were several Scotsmen fixing up an exhibition.

'Glasgow?' I asked.

'Yes,' they replied.

They said that at the time of Suez they had seriously thought of going home, to help the old country. I never found out quite what they would have done.

The girl and I went on. I must have been talking in a very high-flown manner, because at one point she said, 'You know, you ought to start a crusade.' This again gave me the feeling that I could save the world.

We took a crowded bus up a hill above San Francisco. We peered into an ashen church, where a priest in glasses was haranguing a sad-looking congregation over a metallic public address system; it was intimidating; when they came to sing a hymn, the music sounded as though it was canned. At last the girl gave me a dollar, and left me.

I wandered into a park full of large, broad-leaved trees. In the middle of the park was a picture gallery that had been founded by a millionaire: it seemed to me that all the old masters in the gallery were fakes. The last room of the gallery was full of weapons past and present, and I had the impression that they turned up the heat in this last room, varying it from hot to very hot, so that it was oppressive and the memory of the dull black weapons stayed with the culture-seekers after every visit. Outside the gallery I ran into a young Negro. We walked and talked. We reached the doors of a planetarium, and sat on the steps outside in the sun, watching a tank full of piranha, those small tropical fish that can strip a man of his flesh.

I went back down the hill to the centre of San Francisco, and wandered the streets in the pink evening light. The bars were crowded. Suddenly someone called my name: I looked up, and there, sitting at tables outside a café, were the NATO journalists. I rejoined them.

The next day the group's junior conducting officer, the high-pitched young man in glasses, and I flew to Chicago. The town was covered in snow. I stayed with Adrian, whom I had not seen for several years. He had a room with a bath in a low building. It was good to see him.

In Chicago I saw some of the buildings of Mies Van der Rohe, which struck me as sinister, like the hives of insects. Someone arranged for me to meet Nelson Algren, the writer ('there's something I want to ask you,' Algren said on the telephone); but the junior conducting officer whirled me round town on the afternoon I was to meet Algren, and, to my shame, I forgot about the appointment. The junior conducting officer took me on a tour of Marshall Field's, the great store, which struck me as a kind of nightmare Harrods. Afterwards, on a cold evening, we tried to find a taxi. At last the junior conducting officer waved one down, I said goodnight to him, and climbed in. The taxi had not gone far before it stopped and a very rough-looking red-haired man scrambled in. I could make nothing of this. We drove on for a bit, and then I turned to the red-haired man and said 'Right. Get out. *Get out.*' The taxi pulled up, and the man climbed out. To this day I have never understood the episode.

In order that I could leave America, Adrian arranged for the British Consul to give me in place of my passport a stamped paper bearing my photograph. My passport was still in the left-luggage office of Los Angeles station. Before BOAC would fly me, I had to have clearance from a psychiatrist. Adrian took me to an enclosed, brightly-lit clinic, where two psychiatrists in high-collared white jackets buttoned up the front bore down on me. The psychiatrists and I talked. One of them was young and bald and wore rimless glasses.

'Does he always reply so fast? Fizz, fizz, fizz, snap, snap, snap?' the elder psychiatrist asked Adrian of me.

'Yes, I think he does,' Adrian said.

The elder psychiatrist had a dark moustache and belonged to some Anglo-U.S. society.

They did not lock me up in the clinic. I continued to stay with Adrian. But I talked of 'them' and 'us'. 'They' tended to wear thick-lensed glasses and were like insects. 'We' were the good and the true. Catholic priests and Negroes were on our side. I had to visit the elder psychiatrist once more in his office high in a sky-scraper. I felt, as I sat in the waiting room glancing at a magazine, that it was essential to preserve a normal front. People might be observing me. I went in to see the psychiatrist, and again we talked. Suddenly he said, 'Right, now tell me all about it.'

I told him of the houses in El Paso that were just façades, made of wood, paint, and plaster, as though for a film set; I told him of my hotel room in El Paso that seemed to grow smaller and to close in on me. 'They were out to get me,' I said.

'I see,' said the psychiatrist, stroking his chin.

I launched into a passionate attack on America and the American way of life.

'I wouldn't say that's all *quite* true,' the psychiatrist said.

Adrian accompanied me back to England. The runways of Chicago airport were covered in hard snow. We flew in a Britannia. When I reached home I found that Jill had not, despite my telephone call from San Francisco, returned the television set.

I found a Christmas card waiting on my desk at the paper. It was from the bald Greek journalist, whose shoes I had admired in Washington.

'A pair of good Greek shoes is still in your disposition', the card said. 'Please send me your measures'.

I sent my measurements. A few days later a pair of Thessalonikan suède shoes arrived, with an accompanying letter:

My very dear Friend,
I send you your shoes, made by my own shoemaker with a special care and according to your measurements.

As most steps of the Londoners are steps in the fog, and the sky over there is somehow, thus the soil becoming slippery, I thought it advisable to have the sole of your shoes covered by a special crêpe with a rough surface, which will help you to be allways standing on your feet and to avoid any unvoluntary plunge.

It will be a source of you to me if you like them and if they impresse your friends and colleagues.

I greet you with my feelings.
Yours,
Dem. Saphiropoulos

The shoes were too tight; but from sentiment I wore them till they died.

In the following months I cannot have been easy to live with. Jill and my children stood it: I am not sure how. I took to holding up every envelope to the light before posting it, to make sure the letter was inside. I thought endlessly about a remark my father had made just before he married again. His second wife was Jewish.

'My grandmother was French and had Jewish blood,' my father had said.

I mentioned that I might have Jewish blood at a dinner party, when someone said something that teetered on the edge of anti-semitism.

'And the question is,' I said, 'if I do have Jewish blood, would it have been sufficient to qualify me for the chimney if the Germans had invaded England in the last war?'

I was overdoing it a bit.

'My grandmother always said there was nothing better than a little Jewish blood,' the anti-semite replied jocularly.

I have wondered if my own preoccupation with this subject was not itself a form of anti-semitism.

'Why can't you be more natural and take things in a straightforward way?' Jill would say to me.

That summer my father died. On the day of his cremation at the crematorium near my home I lunched with my stepmother and her father, a devout Jew. Over lunch the conversation for some reason turned to Nazi Germany.

'No man who is not German should say he would not have been a Nazi,' I said. 'By the law of averages I almost certainly would have been a Nazi had I been German. How dare I say otherwise?'

I regretted the remark, for it deeply upset my stepmother's father. After that day he scarcely spoke to me again during his lifetime. We drove to the crematorium in his Rolls-Royce, and I thought how high the bonnet seemed.

We went once more on holiday to Cornwall. The feeling that I had done nothing in my life came to me when I stepped out of the bungalow just before supper on a misty evening. There was a patch of springy grass in front of the bungalow which ended at the tufted overhang of the low cliff leading to the beach. The grass gave out a certain smell which, it seemed, only salt-resilient grass near a cliff could give out, on an evening when there was a sea-mist. It was a sad smell, slightly musty, yet hopeful. Gulls were mewing, and despite the mist there was a breeze. I realized that the last time I had felt like this I was about eleven, on holiday in Dorset before the war. It suddenly seemed that nothing had happened in between. I couldn't say at that moment that I had changed in any way.

I walked to the tufted crest of the cliff, and looked down over the damp beach. The tide was far out, and purple-grey breakers were rolling in out of the grey sea below the grey sky. I listened to them for several minutes. They were rolling in out of the shifting grey, saying, in their own way, that life would go on.

I had bare feet, and sand clung to my salt-sticky ankles. I stepped on some prickly plant, and removed a small thorn from the soft part of my big toe. I bent down and touched my toes three times, took some deep breaths, stretched, turned, and wandered back to the bungalow.

I wondered whether to have a bathe to justify eating a large supper. I only wondered, because I knew perfectly well that I was not going to have a bathe. Instead, I polished a pair of slippers, and then went into the bedroom. Jill was bathing the children next door. I opened the top drawer of the chest of drawers, and took out a bent envelope containing something. I opened the envelope and took out a bedraggled cigar: it was the cigar my father had given me to give to the American, Herb, when Herb and I were planning to cross Algeria with the rebels. The dark green outer skin of the cigar had come unwound and was flaking off, and the cigar had been slightly smoked. I, who had almost never smoked in my life, had been experimenting. I peeled off the outer skin and cut off the smoked tip of the cigar, so that it looked quite respectable. The mouth-end was dark and a bit chewed from previous smoking.

I lit up and took a few experimental puffs; I puffed lightly, looking at myself in the mirror and watching carefully to see if I was blowing out any smoke; I put the cigar in my mouth and chewed on it; then I turned a little, so that my face and the cigar were in profile. I heard the bathroom door open, and quickly took the cigar out of my mouth and thrust it into the top drawer of the chest of drawers with my socks.

Jill came into the room hurriedly, looking for the children's pyjamas. She glanced at me suspiciously.

'What are you doing?' she asked.

'Nothing,' I said. 'Thinking. I've got to write to the bank.'

'Have you done that tea washing-up?' Jill asked.

She hurried out of the room.

I opened the drawer again. A piece of ash had fallen on to a pair of socks, and the cigar had gone out. I smelled the cigar and put it back in the envelope, which I buried beneath the socks. I closed the drawer and left the room, taking one more quick glance at myself in the mirror. I started to hum, and went into the kitchen to wash up the tea things.

After my holiday, Jane, a photographer, and I were sent to Blackpool. One sunny afternoon we walked down the pier and watched fishermen catching plaice.

'See that man over there in a baseball cap and glasses?' I said to Jane. 'He looks just like Epstein, doesn't he?'

Jane agreed. She had met Epstein several times.

We walked back from the end of the pier, and by the turnstiles we saw an evening paper hoarding: 'Epstein dead.'

The man that looked like Epstein had vanished.

We then visited some of Epstein's great figures in the basement of a Blackpool waxworks. To reach the basement we passed the grinning effigies of royalty and of tiny, bitter jockeys. A jukebox howled. We gazed up at Epstein's figures: they were powerful: one of them, I remember, gave me a feeling of how Adam had given birth, had spontaneously generated Eve.

Back in London I began to get a fuzzy feeling in my feet; a feeling that was almost sour. I never slept. I shouted at men in pubs that they didn't need their hearing-aids.

People with glasses were sinister: there was a plot, and they were behind it; they were burning up the world. Deserts, I thought, were dead, and so was the oil beneath. Cars were like insects, humming in the night. I tore up a *Time Magazine* that had a cover picture of Soustelle. The magazine belonged to a friend, who slapped my face in a fury. I pinned his arms and said: 'I mean no harm. But Soustelle is evil.'

It was sunny when I walked home from the Underground on the evening of the same day. When I reached the gates of the crematorium they were open, and a sign said, 'Visitors Welcome'. I went in – past the ashen chapel and the oriental red-brick palace with a central tower that has a green copper cupola and two windows like eyes – through an open door in a wall, and out into the gardens of remembrance with their spacious lawns. I had not seen these gardens at my father's cremation. I walked over the grass until I came to an ornamental Japanese pond with a bridge upon which were tablets bearing the names of the dead. I noticed a very fresh tablet with the name of a member of Parliament I had thought to be still alive. (My father had forbidden any nonsense: no mourning, no tablet, no flowers.)

On the grass near the Japanese pond I saw a green plastic hose. I walked over to the green plastic hose and tied a knot in it: I pulled the knot as tight as I could.

Then I walked back across the lawns and entered the ashen chapel. Here I smashed one or two urns and in their place put half-a-crowns, with the Queen's head upwards. This was to symbolize my view that death, burial and cremation should be free for all the people represented by the Queen.

Leaving the chapel, I shouted at a uniformed attendant, who cringed. I walked home down the white lines in the centre of the road.

In bed that night, inspired by Epstein's view of how Adam had spontaneously generated Eve, I practised weird yogic exercises, which alarmed Jill.

The next day, a Saturday, I walked out of the office at lunchtime. The weather was still fine, and I wanted to sit on the pavement. But some workmen with pneumatic drills distracted me. I hated cars at this time. I went up to the Irish foreman, took over his pneumatic drill, and started attacking the asphalt in an effort to make a trench across the road, and thus stop all traffic: I wanted the workmen and the foreman to follow my example; they were long-suffering, but unimpressed.

Eventually a large Daimler hire-car came down the slope and stopped at the T-junction near us: I can see that Daimler now, black and massive, with white wedding streamers from windscreen to bonnet, as it halted below the blue-and-gold sign of a pub. The Irish foreman said, 'Here's a car for to get in; I tink dat's best for you.' He opened the Daimler's door, and I bounded in, hopeful.

The driver, thin and uniformed, anonymous in a cap on the other side of the glass partition, did not stir, though he must have known I was there. He moved off smoothly and turned up Fleet Street from Ludgate Circus. He didn't seem to want to get me out of the car. He was taking me to the bride.

The bride was standing in a side entrance of the *News of the World* wearing a white dress adorned with orange-blossom. Her father, a small, grey-haired caretaker of the *News of the World*, held her hand. She was small and quiet and ready for the sacrifice.

She and her father did not seem surprised to see me bound out of the back of their bridal Daimler. The three of us climbed into the back of the great car, and swept round to St Bride's, only a few yards away. I climbed out early, somehow, and stood in a prominent position in the church, welcoming them in, very stern, with important gestures. During the marriage service I stood or sat near the organist, a pleasant, contained man, wearing a Press Club tie. I whispered to him between hymns, telling him the organ was not playing quite true. He took it very well.

One of the paper's drivers took me home that afternoon. I wanted him to have a cup of tea and eat bread and honey in the sun with my family on our small front lawn.

The next day a Doctor Plowright came to the house. He was tall, thin, and sensitive. He listened to me.

'They're burning up the world,' I said. 'Taking out all its goodness. And if they take out too much, the world may fly to pieces.'

'You are very, very ill,' Dr Plowright told me.

He gave me some bomb-shaped blue pills, which were meant

to knock me out. When he left, I walked out with him to his car.

'Plow-right,' I said to him. 'Well, it's a good old English name: straight lines. I trust you.'

He looked serious.

'Tell me, doctor,' I said. 'What is the difference between life and death? After all, your beard still grows after death.'

Dr Plowright eyed me sternly: 'It doesn't grow for long, you know,' he said.

He drove away.

The next day they took me, heavily drugged, to the clinic near London Bridge Station run by the Television Psychiatrist. I was a 'voluntary patient'.

'Damn me if I haven't wound up in the nuthouse,' I thought.

In the clinic they tried to put me to sleep for a fortnight. I dimly remember nurses giving me a blanket-bath and asking me why I was sunburnt. The doctors injected me with vitamins from huge syringes. Once a Polish male nurse called Mr Z twisted my arm.

'You do what we want here,' he said.

After they had tried putting me to sleep for a fortnight, they wanted to give me electric shock. But I would not sign the paper agreeing to this. They drugged me. At night the ceiling light was blue, and they could gaze in at me through a sort of glass porthole in the door of my room.

'You are very ill, all revved up,' a small, dominating consultant told me on my thirty-fourth birthday. 'You're going to stay here a *very* long time.'

I still had that sour, fuzzy feeling in my feet.

I painted a picture for my children on the back of an envelope: it was of a small Chinese girl with pigtails who was picking flowers against a red sunset near a Chinese house with a roof that turned up at the eaves like the prow of a Viking ship.

I tried, with the help of a young nurse, to make the key of life, the clay shape that had to be made. The nurse was a wonderful, patient girl. When I was paralysed by drugs she bathed me.

They lent me a gramophone, and I wound it up laboriously

and put on records of Vera Lynn given me by the small cockney grandson of a woman patient.

Once I ran into the Television Psychiatrist in a corridor when he was showing round a party of German or Swedish visitors.

'Hullo,' I said. 'Do you remember we were on television? You told me you thought that if you had had Christ on your couch you would have recognized him.'

The Television Psychiatrist didn't remember me. He owned a chocolate-coloured Bentley.

After a time I was able to go up on the flat roof of the clinic. Two painters were at work up there. They were painting from cradles slung over the side of the building, and they thought nothing of heights. They were both Battersea men: Mr A. J. Gurney and Mr George Simpson, known as 'Curly'. Mr Gurney was using a pointed, worn brush that 'cut in' well. He had tried using a paint roller on the thick wire grille surrounding the flat roof, but it was no good. I got to know the two men quite well. They said they had both lived in the same house in Battersea during the big flood of 1928. Gurney had been ABA feather-weight champion. He was with the parachutists at Arnhem, and broke both legs when landing: in England he was given electric shock to get over it.

'If he can get over it,' I thought, 'so can I.'

'Curly' Simpson told me he had eight children and was a lapsed Catholic. He was always humming 'Murray Mints, Murray Mints,' as he painted the pipes with bitumen.

Two other good men working at the clinic and the great hospital to which it belonged were the window cleaners, Mr Charles Phillips senior and his son, Mr Charles Phillips junior. Mr Charles Phillips senior had been cleaning the windows of the hospital from six-thirty in the morning till three-thirty in the afternoon for fifty-one years.

'Enjoy it?' he said in answer to my question. 'It's a case of used to it. It comes naturally.'

He used only water, chammy leather, and a damp cloth.

'The chammy leather seems very dirty, but it's capable of doing its job,' he said.

I used to watch him standing outside calmly on high window-sills and cleaning methodically. He used no safety harness.

After a time they seemed to increase the drugs I was taking: the drugs made me bow down on the floor like a praying mantis. One night, under the glowing blue ceiling light, I was again paralysed and felt very ill. The night-sister came in to me: she sent for a doctor, who sent for the consultant at three in the morning.

'I can't live,' I managed to say.

They took off the drugs, or possibly gave me an antidote. At last I could stand up, and I stamped out, swearing, into the passage. They put me in a padded, soundproof room. I noticed that someone had blown his nose on the padding.

'God,' I said to the consultant a day or two later, 'I felt like hell that night you came out and took the drugs off.'

'It was very unpleasant for all of us,' he replied.

When Jill visited me one evening, I said: 'Get me out of here, have me home, or we divorce.'

It upset her very much and, to protect her, the doctors did not allow her to visit me for some time. I sent her messages through my brother Andy, who visited me regularly.

'Tell her I will forgive her for not returning the television set,' I said, 'if she will forgive me for being unfaithful to her when I was abroad.'

I was scarcely offering a fair exchange.

I told Andy and my mother that I would like, astonishingly, to see a parson. My mother spoke to the Bishop of Southwark, who came, wearing sombre black, to see me twice. It was kind of him. But by then I did not feel so in need of a parson. I said almost nothing during his visits.

I became paralysed with drugs again, and they took me in a wheelchair for an encephalogram reading. A neurologist examined my reflexes.

The food in the clinic was bad and there were silver fish in the napkins.

Battle of Britain Day came, and, lying in bed, drugged, I heard an old Spitfire turning in the evening sky above St Paul's. I could almost smell the bitterness of the cockpit. It seemed to me that I had flown in another life, and had died when I had crashed into pylons in the fog.

I got better, but the days dragged. We had to shave with an electric razor, not a blade, and the one razor served many patients. The patients had to do the housework, and I raved to the day sister about the dangers of using silicone floor polish.

'It's dead,' I said.

A small, fat Indian patient heard me, and said: 'Mr Gale, you are very wise man.'

There was a beautiful Pakistani girl patient who had had a leucotomy and was uncontrolled: her father was very rich, and she walked about ceaselessly and cried all day about the poor. A woman sang 'Tell Him You Love Him'. On grey days a girl played a flute in the hospital laboratories opposite.

One day the consultant said he thought a bit of electric shock would do me good: 'Just to give you a boost.'

So I agreed.

At last, after four months in the clinic, I was discharged. Jill came to fetch me.

'Come on, hurry up,' she said, in a businesslike way, 'we're pushed for time.'

Lying in bed one night at home, I thought of the Mauser machine-pistol and its seventy rounds of ammunition that I had brought back from Germany at the end of the war: the Mauser was in the loft: it could be a way out.

But the next morning Kiki, our youngest daughter, came into our room and climbed into our bed.

'I was laughing in the night,' she said. 'I dreamed Father Christmas gave me a lilo.'

At about this time there was an amnesty for arms: the public was asked to hand them in.

I took the Mauser of dark blue oiled steel from the loft with its box of ammunition and drove to the nearest police station. A friend was with me. He examined the Mauser as we drove along.

'Isn't it rather a pity to hand it in?' he said. 'It is the most beautiful thing.'

'Well,' I said. 'It's not beautiful to me.'

A policeman behind the counter took the Mauser and counted the ammunition.

'There are sixty-three rounds,' the policeman said. 'Not seventy.'

He asked me to sign a form.

We left the police station. It was the most beautiful day.